Framing Play Design

Framing Play Design
© 2020 Sune Gudiksen, Helle Marie Skovbjerg and BIS Publishers

Cover photo: Ane Gleerup
Graphic design, cover design and illustrations: Strunge Grafik

BIS Publishers
Building Het Sieraad
Postjesweg 1
1057 DT Amsterdam
The Netherlands
T +31 (0)20 515 02 30
bis@bispublishers.com
www.bispublishers.com

ISBN 978 90 6369 572 9

Framing Play Design

A Hands-on Guide for Designers, Learners & Innovators

Sune Gudiksen & Helle Marie Skovbjerg

BIS Publishers

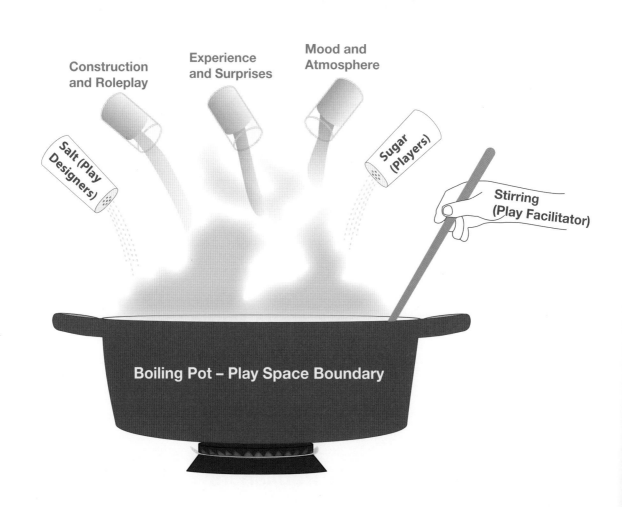

Forewords

This book is one of the early results of a close collaboration between Design School Kolding and The LEGO Foundation, which revolves around a master's programme and a research programme. For this reason, we break with the convention of having only one foreword and present two – one from each collaborator.

By Lene Tanggaard, Rector Design School Kolding, Professor of Educational Psychology

Some years ago, I found myself supervising a PhD student as I had done so many times before. The co-supervisor joined our meeting, and we agreed we felt a bit stuck with too much and too unstructured research data. Furthermore, we were lacking in ideas on how to tackle the situation and the problems it evidently caused for the progress of the project and for the PhD student. Because of this, or for some other reason, we suddenly found ourselves laughing, joking about hydroplanes and how everybody should allow themselves to try one, at least once in their lifetime. Eventually, the co-supervisor commented on our detour saying that we all have to remember to have fun as part of our working lives. It was fun and what is more, we found a solution to our problem. We just had to allow our thoughts to fly away for a little while. The situation taught me how effective playing with your imagination can be in a serious situation, but it also reminded me of the basic qualities in life and our abilities as humans. Play can help us to grow, throughout life if we are open to it, and allow us to envision new realities using our imagination to create scenarios for improvisation.

In your hands, or on your screen, you now have a wonderful and diversified book on play design. As stated in the prologue, the book is "a primer on applied play design for designers, learners and innovators and covers Northern European play design practice and its unique qualities".

From my perspective, the combination of play and design adds something very valuable to our common understanding of design, and specifically Nordic design. The book draws a line back to a year-long tradition for user-driven, participatory co-design in Europe. This tradition is somehow 'understated', building upon unique, functional and aesthetic qualities. However, play adds something odd or even radical to this tradition. Play is imaginative. It takes us beyond the here-and-now. It allows us to experiment with alternatives and to transport ourselves into an imaginary setting. As most of us have been raised with moving images, the next generations are used to constructing interactive sceneries most markedly through digital computer games. It is therefore not surprising that play design is rapidly making its way into a number of fields and industries. Nevertheless, play design is more than a discipline. It is a mind-set, a way of existing in the world, as well as a mood creator.

Play design can and will change the world. On the Danish Broadcasting Corporation's evening news Sunday the 26th of April, medical researcher Anders Fomsgaard, a specialist in virology, said in an interview concerning the Corona crisis in 2020 that he always asks new researchers whether they want to become Nobel Prize winners or whether they want to change the world. Fomsgaard believes in the true value of research and so he aspires for the latter, and I guess many play designers and play design researchers share his approach. In the hands of the right people, play design can do good in the world. Play design represents faith in people and the power of our imaginative abilities. It is fun, but serious fun!

Play is spontaneous, yet sometimes guided by rules. It can be wild, speculative – it lets people fly without wings, it is a corrective to instrumentalism, and it is almost impossible to imagine organisms playing while being cynical.

Designers are agents of holistic change. I firmly believe that play design represents the next generation of Nordic design. It combines the understated with the imaginative, allowing the world to change in ways that benefit its inhabitants by bridging the multiplicity and ambiguity of technical, economic, social, cultural and sustainability-related aspects and providing sometimes physical, relatable manifestations of this.

Enjoy the reading.

By Bo Stjerne Thomsen, PhD, Vice-President and Chair of Learning through Play, The LEGO Foundation

The world would benefit from a deeper understanding of the value of play and play design. We need a shared language to articulate its benefits, and we need to design applications to shape action and embed playful experiences in practice. This publication aims to do so. It is the work of an extraordinary group one should look out for in the coming years – the Design for Play collective of researchers and practitioners springing from the Design School Kolding in Denmark, and its far-reaching international network.

The compilation of examples illustrates how uniquely important play is in the 21st century; not only as a process, which is apparently different from everyday life, but as an approach which shapes the interactions and environments of our future lives. These insights bring together the multiple theories behind play and design, and describe the ingredients and core understanding needed in order to equip designers, innovators, facilitators, students and researchers with a refreshing framework for theorising and practising play design.

This will shape how we design our environments and the role of the facilitator as mediator between design and participants, in order to bring all of us a step closer to being more playful and curious on our journey of lifelong learning.

The LEGO Foundation takes great inspiration in this work and is proud of a long-standing partnership with Design School Kolding to further extend the importance of play, and ensure a new generation of play designers and researchers can empower children to become creative, engaged, lifelong learners.

Over the years, we have brought together our international partners to emphasize how the playful experience is equipping us with the essential skills for the future (Zosh et al. 2017), and changing education to recognize the importance of learning through play (Parker & Thomsen 2019). In this publication, this view is further refined and expanded to emphasize that knowledge is shaped by our creativity and playfulness, and design is the best of our human abilities to improve the world we live in, and the opportunities we provide for the next generation.

Enjoy!

Parker, R. & Thomsen, B.S. (2019). Learning through Play at School. LEGO Foundation. Retrieved at: LEGO Foundation https://www.legofoundation.com/media/1687/learning-through-play-school.pdf

Zosh, J. N., Hopkins, E. J., Jensen, H., Liu, C., Neale, D., Hirsh-Pasek, K., & Whitebread, D. (2017). Learning through play: a review of the evidence. LEGO Foundation. Retrieved at: https://www.legofoundation.com/media/1063/learning-through-play_web.pdf

CONTENT

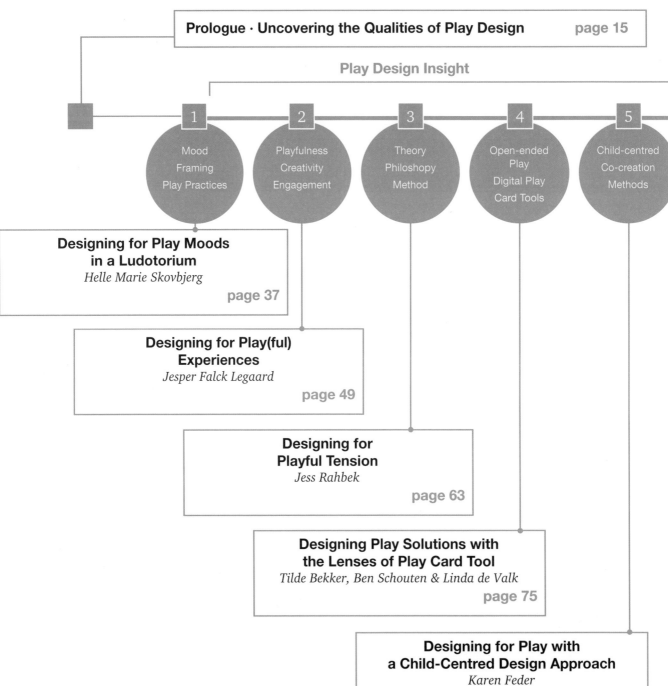

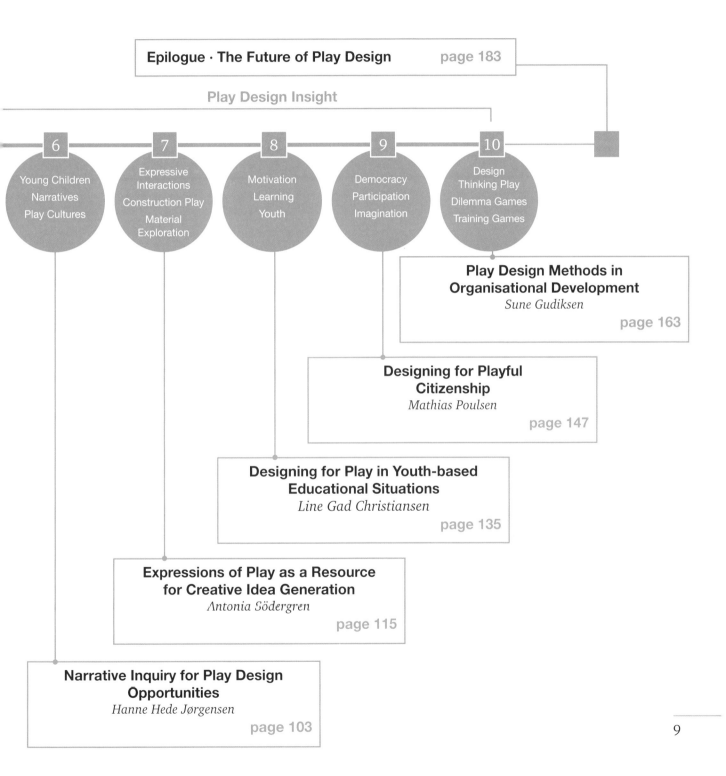

Epilogue · The Future of Play Design

Play Design Insight

6
Young Children
Narratives
Play Cultures

7
Expressive
Interactions
Construction Play
Material
Exploration

8
Motivation
Learning
Youth

9
Democracy
Participation
Imagination

10
Design
Thinking Play
Dilemma Games
Training Games

Preface

This book aims to demonstrate that the application of play design is gaining favour as a way of creating meaningful experiences, reaching participant-led learning objectives and accessing development opportunities in organisations and institutions. The book provides a set of principles, operational guidelines and first cues to create play design that matters, has an impact on lifelong learning and creates memorable experiences for all participants, leading to new ways of understanding and approaching relationships, practices and ways of living.

This book is a primer on applied play design for designers, learners and innovators and covers European play design practice and its unique qualities. Ultimately, we hope to initiate conversations on a variety of perspectives for play design in general and generate opportunities for a series of related books from international communities. Play design is something of a lost art that should be explored in order to discover a number of domains in which play may be applied for a variety of different purposes.

MIT professor and multiple award-winning game designer Eric Zimmerman claimed in 2013 that this century will be defined by play and games and that 'information has been put on play' (Zimmerman 2013). In the 20th century, he observed, the moving image was the dominant cultural form, but in the 21st century play and games are replacing linear media and traditional one-way communication. The last five years have only confirmed this rapid development.

In the introduction to his ground-breaking book *The Ambiguity of Play*, prominent play researcher Brian Sutton-Smith stated that, while trying to understand play theoretically, we often descend into silliness (Sutton-Smith 2001). In this book, we attempt to understand play design and play situations, accepting the risk of descending into silliness, but insisting on the importance of having a language that combines a theoretical and practical mindset (moving between abstract and concrete levels of thought) for the development of specific play designs. Play design is more than merely the idea of the functionality and practical usefulness of play but is a matter related to our existence, to the experience of being alive as a human being in all types of situations.

Play design as a field of practice cannot be isolated to a specific sector or for that matter a specific age, nor can play designers be categorized in a limited way. As with any design, one can learn skills and build up competencies to improve and acquire a sense of detail for creating, designing or orchestrating prompts and triggers for play activities. Although play design is not confined to a specific sector, we consider here three broad target groups – designers, learners and innovators – who are possible first-movers in the development and expansion of play practices.

Designers

Designers create all sorts of play design, including those from the toy and game entertainment industry, which has grown so rapidly in recent years. Industrial and interior designers focus on playgrounds, workspaces, museum spaces and so on, where play interaction may be a stand-out ingredient. Product, service and social designers add play elements to their core products as experiential components, giving them competitive advantages or even leading to societal changes. The trend is for product designers and service providers to move towards the integration of more play-related interaction principles and user influence. Sustainability-oriented designers and practitioners seek to use play design as part of a set of connected activities that change behaviours. Communication design depends on new devices, digital technology infrastructure and media formats that create opportunities for highly engaging, interactive, or ludic, formats that are immersive.

Learners

Play connected to learning situations is receiving renewed attention from practitioners including teachers, trainers, facilitators and instructors involved in learning activities in a wide range of contexts, such as schools and higher education establishments, museums and other knowledge institutions and in the field of continuing education and competence development in organizations. At the heart of *learner-centred* and *experiential* learning approaches lies an orientation towards play interaction. Trainers, teachers and instructors are increasingly moving away from instructivism, involving one-way communication, and towards a multitude of learner-centred, play-oriented activities to encourage deeper learning.

Innovators

Organizations, both private and public, are starting to include play elements in their development processes and in the search for new sorts of products, services and experiences. This group may be even more process-oriented than the previous two groups. What they are creating may not be 'play design product'-like, but they may use play as a step in their design, innovation and change processes and as a way to involve and engage cross-disciplinary users, stakeholders and clients. Using play as vehicle for exploration leads to the reframing of problems and solutions, and develops a mindset of curiosity and the skill to work around complex problems. Such attitudes and skills are sought after at a time when markets are changing rapidly and working practices need to adapt accordingly.

Students, Teachers and Researchers in Higher Education

Among all three target groups, there are students, teachers and researchers seeking a key resource to add to the course literature. In Europe and around the world – the US, Canada, Australia, South Korea, Singapore, India, among others – higher education institutions are increasingly picking, up themes around play design and including them in their curricula. In addition, new research groups with a point of departure in applied play practice are flourishing.

We begin by revealing the main qualities found in play design with references to the following ten chapters written from contributors within the Design-for-Play Group at Design School Kolding in Kolding, Denmark. Each of the ten chapters provides a specific *play design insight* with supporting examples and guidelines. As a reader, you can choose to jump to chapters that seem most relevant to the domain you are working in, but we suggest you also dip at random into other chapters where you may learn about play design principles that you were not aware of and that can have an impact on your practice. Turn to the list of contents, close your eyes and point to somewhere on the page. Open your eyes and follow the section identified, which is a potentially serendipitous choice.

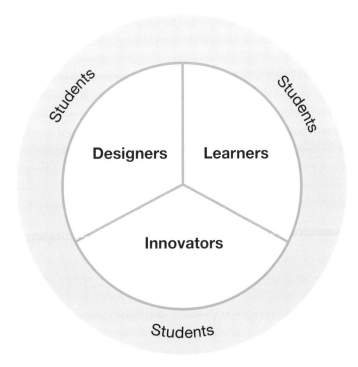

Figure 0.1: Illustrating reader groups

Prologue
Uncovering the Qualities of Play Design

Sune Gudiksen & Helle Marie Skovbjerg

For some decades and in many circles, play has been regarded as being outside learning spheres and only meant for children up to a certain age. Now what can be observed is a revival of the characteristics and potentials of strong play experiences across lifelong learning target groups and in applied situations, as well as broadly in the product, service and experience development industry. Play can have an extremely positive effect on participants and surroundings.

Play design qualities are strongly linked to participants because they represent qualities *to somebody* (Skovbjerg 2018; Gadamer 2013). If the participants do not relate to the play qualities and find them relevant to their play activity, then their interest will wane. Some play quality examples are: being able to determine one's own path, engaging just for the sake of exploration, exposing oneself to a series of surprises and fostering one's imagination. Product developers and educators need to constantly explore the play qualities of participants. Moreover, the play qualities that can be identified through the knowledge we have about children's play and forms of activities are not necessarily the same as the play qualities to be found among adults. We need to have sensitivity to the diversity of play qualities *to somebody* and be able to design for that diversity.

Participants play a main role in understanding and developing play qualities, which are not static, but instead dynamic and situated. Design is destined to engage participants who will value the qualities of what we have designed. Design has for many years taken the form of participatory design or co-design (Simonsen & Robertson 2012; Sanders & Stappers 2008; Buur & Matthews 2008; Ehn 1993) and there is a strong tradition in Scandinavia for working with design in close collaboration with users and stakeholders. Co-design and participatory design processes are relevant ways to get stakeholders in a specific development project to experience play qualities first-hand.

We argue that play design consists of a mixture of elements. Let us imagine we have a boiling hot cooking pot of play design influences (see Figure 0.2), in which we have:

The pot: The ludic space boundary – this is the temporal world of imagination that is created through play activities. Such a space is not entirely separate from reality but creates a distance from reality, far enough to explore new meanings.

Salt and sugar: Play designers could be seen as the salt and players as the sugar. Both are needed for high-quality play design. On the one hand, players can invent their own play activities, but, on the other hand, they may not move beyond their own circles of imagination if they engage only in self-initiated play activities. It is here suggested that play designers, through all sorts of prompts and triggers, can help players activate such new imaginative states.

Five key ingredients: Five key ingredients seem to be present in most high-quality play design activities: (1) metaphors and narratives that often turn into bigger story worlds; (2) rules and procedures that dictate how the play proceeds, whether these are created before or during play; (3) materials and technologies used in a specific play situation – these create object affordances and constraints that lead the play towards specific meanings; (4) challenges in the play activity and feedback loops occurring as a result; and (5) participation and position – which puts participants in the driving seat and challenge them to explore other angles, perspectives and positions.

Stirring the pot: The pot often needs stirring to turn it into a good dish including play designers, players and sometimes a play design facilitator or play experience facilitator. A key difference between some other design disciplines and play design is that play develops in use and is not just a one-off deliverable. It is design-after-design – in a sense, a full play circle.

Three flavours: Three key flavours can be traced in the history of play, though not all of them are always foregrounded in all play activities: (1) mood and atmosphere; (2) experience and surprise; and (3) construction with role play.

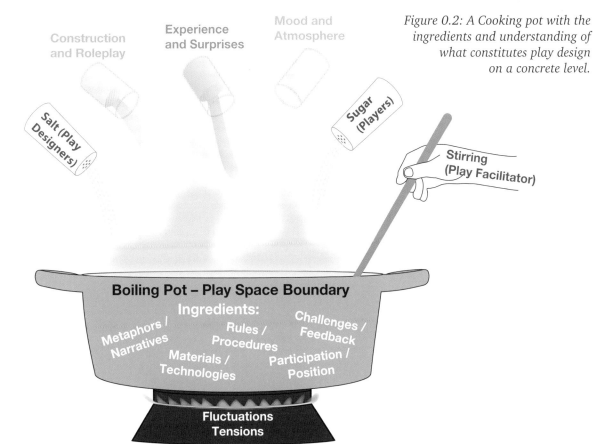

Figure 0.2: A Cooking pot with the ingredients and understanding of what constitutes play design on a concrete level.

17

The Boiling Pot –
the Play Space Boundary

Play activity takes place in frame that differs from everyday life, where movements, words and the things around us can be perceived as taking on meanings other than their 'normal' meanings, often referred to as the magic circle. There is much debate about this 'magic circle'. As pioneering play researcher Johan Huizinga (1949) described, it is a (virtual) playground in which special rules apply. He further argued that magic circles are 'temporary worlds within the ordinary world, dedicated to the performance of an act apart' (Huizinga 1949).

The anthropologist Gregory Bateson (1996) argued that the production of meaning in play activity differs from meaning generated outside it. Words and actions in play are a different reality and can have connotations that are not the same as words and actions outside play. 'Framing' was Bateson´s term for activity described as 'this is play' and separated from something that is not play.

In the context of game design, Salen and Zimmerman (2004) argued that, within the magic circle, specific meanings can emerge. Building on the experiential learning model in which learning is a result of concrete experiences, reflective observations, abstract conceptualization and active experimentation, Kolb (1984) and Kolb and Kolb (2010) suggested that the

ludic learning space is the highest form of experiential learning. This space is characterized by principles such as freedom to play, the chaos of uncertainty, welcoming foolishness and stepping out of real life. Such a space has the ability to 'encourage learners to take charge of their own learning based on their own standards of excellence'. Vygotsky (1967) argued that in play 'a new relationship is created between the semantic and visible fields – that is, between situations in thought and real situations'. It can be argued that the essence of the play space lies in allowing uncertainty to exist and embracing changes that emerge from following the logic and references within that space.

Throughout this book, arranging this play space boundary is discussed as the first principle. Helle Marie Skovbjerg (Ch. 1), in her description of setting up a lab format for play design exploration, claims that diving into participants' own play experiences is a way to create a safe space and access personal reflections and that the subsequent activities have a higher degree of ownership. Antonia Södergren (Ch. 7) argues that gaining trust and a feeling of safety for pre-schoolers is crucial. Likewise, Line Christiansen (Ch. 8) states that it is vital to remove or downplay some of the social insecurity found in all types of classroom settings. Sune Gudiksen (Ch. 10) argues that the boundary is not as well demarcated as one might hope when it comes to such a play space – everyday life and reality pop up from time to time, even when one has reached a high level of an imaginative state, but this everyday life and current understanding of the world can be suspended to some degree during these activities. Mathias Poulsen (Ch. 9) explains, in relation to what he dubs *small democracy*, that, to allow for everyday democratic encounters and participant agency, establishing trust is vital. This, he suggests, becomes the main purpose, if not the sole purpose of being immersed in play.

These contributions contain some common threads. First, through *trust* and *safety*, we can begin to relate to those present and understand the perspectives and actions of those who come from a different background, cultural understanding and even thought-world than we do. Second, through these play activities, participants obtain a better knowledge of others and can mirror this in their own way of acting – how they think and react, the underlying perceptions and assumptions and in general how practices are either constituted or transformed.

Influential play and game sociologist Roger Callois (1961) distinguished between paidia (spontaneous play) on the one hand and ludus (formalized and institutionalized play) on the other. Such an opposite or dialectic perspective creates a spectrum

in which various play activities can be categorized based on their design intention and player behaviour. Callois's dialectic between paidia and ludus is still influencing understandings of play today and is being further explored and elaborated.

Writing in several articles in the last decade, Tilde Bekker, Ben Schouten and Linda de Valk (Ch. 4) have helped explain *open-ended play* as being a play format in the middle between paidia and ludus – a sweet spot or balance to aim for in many play designs. As they write (see also Figure 4.2, Ch. 4):

Emergence and strategy are examples of how play scenarios can evolve over time, balancing, opening up and narrowing down the play space and its possible procedures, stories and scenarios

The purpose is not to aim for one end of the spectrum or the other, either paidia or ludus, but to find a balance that may fluctuate a bit but also stays close to the middle.

In Chapter Ten Sune Gudiksen has explored how various play design methods and processes in organisations and learning situations can vary from very open, with few play principles that allow emergent patterns to evolve, to more behavioural play activities that are subject to more rules and procedures (see Figure 10.1, Ch. 10). He distinguishes between design intentions before a specific play activity occurs and then as it evolves. What to aim for depends on the purpose of the play design and the potential participants who will be involved. A *progression-based* and *behavioural-oriented* play design can be strong in situations where routines are to be changed, where participants have to break out of habitual thinking and where more specific paths have to be followed in the activity. An *emergence-based* and *complexity-oriented* structure generates many possible and unpredictable outcomes.

Jess Rahbek (Ch. 3) suggests finding balances or activating tensions between *orderly* and *unruly* elements in the play design and as the play evolves. By way of illustration, he cites a play experience in which it is attempted to hold two magnets together – orderly and unruly play ingredients – that are also repelling each other. This is what he calls *playful tension* (see also Figure 3.2, Ch. 3).

Overall, to create the pot (play space), two overall principles must be considered. First, what kinds of play activities are we aiming for and what is the best fit in the paidia–ludus spectrum? Second, how do we arrange the space in such a way that enough trust and safety are established to create a distance from everyday life? Subsequent chapters give insights into the principles for this, depending on context and situation.

This fluctuation between two poles also points to the dilemma that all play designers may find themselves in from time to time. How much is to be designed and how much is to be developed by the players? What impact can the play designer have in the full play circle? This relates to finding the right amount of *salt* (play design) and *sugar* (player influence).

Salt and Sugar – Play Designers and Players

Play design is particularly good at bringing forth emergent patterns that leave pre-fixed outcomes behind. Play design and the experience one encounters as part of a product or service can strike an effective balance between behavioural design, with elements of triggers, prompts, inventories of materials/technologies and combinatorics, and status-quo thinking – this is what we call *the salt* in the cooking pot. Leaving space for emergent in-play patterns and participants' imaginative thoughts through open-ended play are what we call *the sugar*. Balancing the salt and sugar in a given situation is extremely difficult. Toy companies investigate creating products or inventories of materials, in which the combinatorics and ideas of what to create can be almost endless – incorporating triggers that allow for initial understanding but do not veer towards becoming manuals.

In such toy companies as LEGO and Haba, it is recognized that design should not be too closed or pre-fixed – this is both a way to differentiate and create competitive advantages and a way to allow for more play styles and preferences, while at the same time generating a higher degree of ownership and attachment to the product. Open-ended play is quickly becoming the way in which product companies, museums, tourist attractions and similar organisations activate personalized experiences. Build-a-Bear Workshop, Inc., and Ritter Sport in the early years of the century were among the first companies to experiment with customized and more personalized experiences. The financial crisis starting in 2007 reduced the number of companies working towards such experiences and the coronavirus crisis in 2020 will have a similar effect, but after such crises the industry seems to return to the design of meaningful experiences, with focus less on consumption and more on replayability and re-use, so that a single play design has value for a series of players over time.

During the 1980s and 1990s, video games started to rise in popularity. Owing to the limited power of computers at that time, most games ended up being linear in style, involving moving from level to level. Exceptions could already be found at that time, however, for instance the city-building game *Sim City* was created with an inventory of options but no specific missions or steps to follow, an early example of an open-ended video game.

Such open-ended games acknowledge that most players do not enjoy taking the same pre-fixed journey over and over again. To keep such a game alive for a longer period, the procedure must (beyond maybe a tutorial) be determined by the players. In most computer and mobile games now, there is an increased focus on games in which players can influence their own journeys and choose a number of different directions, roles and materials (equipment/resources) and also jump from being a player to being a maker of new stories, challenges and full levels. The character Super Mario is well known to those who grew up in the 1990s. Within the last five years, Nintendo started to develop *Super Mario Maker* and *Super Mario Maker 2*, which allow players to move beyond playing levels to creating their own unlimited courses that other players can access from across the world. In short, players become makers.

In learning institutions in Scandinavia, there is a move away from pre-fixed learning agendas and the idea that the teacher has all the knowledge. Instead, new perspectives on specific topics are developed throughout sessions, and pupils and students are encouraged to look beyond the current understanding and search for new meaning through play-based learning activities. Activities are becoming experiential and teachers and pedagogues are no longer only proceeding with prepared teaching materials but instead trying to dive directly into the thinking of the pupils and students as new imaginative states occur. A new project, *Playful Learning Research*, run by Design School Kolding, the LEGO Foundation and all university colleges in Denmark (Playful Learning Research 2020), seeks to advance the move away from instructivism with also pre-fixed curricula and learning goals and instead allow for a higher degree of participation and ownership of the content.

When individuals become active participants in their learning, using many of their senses, content and a variety of perspectives on the matter at hand are more easily digested and remembered, as participants create their own system of thoughts in relation to the topic. The discourse found in reports and theories of 21st-century skills centres around four categories of skills – *communication*, *collaboration*, *critical thinking* and *creativity* (Soffel 2016) – and seems to connect well with the typical nature of play activities. Play design could be a factor that can help develop play activities and support the novel framing of problems and ideas in the school system, from public school to higher education. Also, in companies and public institutions, play design becomes an enabler of the new. However, establishing a play boundary in such organisations is extremely difficult, as it requires overcoming years of specific practices, routines, personal interests and fixed

ways of seeing the world (which may indeed have worked for many years). But play can access scenario experimentation beyond the status quo and explore roles, mindsets and working procedures. Pioneer play sociologist Roger Callois (1961) argued that:

An outcome known in advance, with no possibility of error or surprise, clearly leading to an inescapable result, is incompatible with the nature of play.

In all the above-mentioned situations, the creation of these play space boundaries is necessary to allow for uncertainty, building up a capacity to deal with complexity and relate to the participants involved. Situational constraints affects how and in what way the play space can created (See Figure 0.3 for examples on situational constraints). Karen Feder (Ch. 5) argues that this move away from 'I know what the children need and want' or likewise a move away from assumptions in relation to adult connections (whether in work or privately) demands courage and nerve from the players. In situations where outcomes are known in advance, play is unlikely to be the answer, but activities based on known outcomes offer few surprises and can deprive us of the ability to explore life and the conditions and situations in which we are involved.

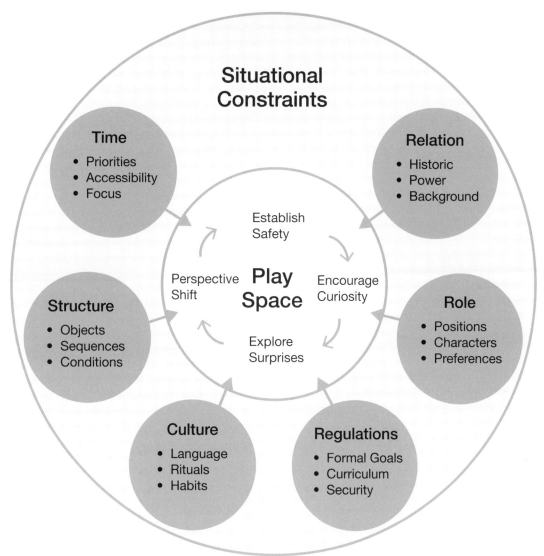

Situational Constraints

Time
- Priorities
- Accessibility
- Focus

Relation
- Historic
- Power
- Background

Structure
- Objects
- Sequences
- Conditions

Role
- Positions
- Characters
- Preferences

Culture
- Language
- Rituals
- Habits

Regulations
- Formal Goals
- Curriculum
- Security

Play Space

Establish Safety

Encourage Curiosity

Explore Surprises

Perspective Shift

Figure 0.3: Play Space Boundaries and the Situational Constraints that Influence the Establishment of the Boundary

Five Key Play Ingredients

Five key ingredients in the 'pot' seem to be more or less present in all accounts in this book. It is through the arrangement of these five key ingredients that players or participants can reach imaginative states and hence all play together in a single play activity.

1. Metaphors and Narratives

As shown in a number of empirical studies over the years, players explore the meaning of an activity in the light of the supporting materials. In video games, there is normally a story, which is a main part of the game – sometimes fully fleshed out with movie sequences and at other times a simple story that will trigger players to start. The story provides potential paths and directions for players to follow but also to shape for themselves. In play design processes, the story can often be more like a metaphor framing new imaginative situations. A specific toy can result in metaphors that over time turn into stories.

A metaphor has been defined as 'a way of conceiving of one thing in terms of another, and its primary function is understanding' (Lakoff 1980). Familiar metaphors create initial understanding and move our thinking away from the status quo. This is what gives initial access to imaginative states. Hanne Hede Jørgensen (Ch. 6) describes a storytelling activity initiated every Friday by teachers in the institutions she follows, called the Mermaid stories. It is an optional but popular choice for children, because they can create mermaids, sharks and other marine creatures, using their imagination in preference to the facts that they know. Similarly, teachers create a play with some rules called *Escape from the Shark*. The teacher takes the role of the shark and the children play the parts of other marine creatures that have to escape.

Sune Gudiksen (Ch. 10) describes an organizational play activity related to creating balance between short-term operational thinking and long-term innovation, which is called *Business Branching* and is based on the idea of trees and growth. All the materials build on this central metaphor, which lets the players quickly grasp meaning and find their own views and interpretations. Jesper Falck Legaard (Ch. 2)

describes a metaphorical reframing of playful work environments using the phrase 'Fire in the hole!' – and through this quickly switching the orientation and mindset of the participants to imagine what the office environment would look like in a pirate world. Mathias Poulsen (Ch. 9) describes how a concept at CounterPlay festival in Denmark called *PowerPoint Karaoke* was invented and used: slide decks would be randomly assigned to a group of presenters, who had to improvise their presentation. Again, participants take a well-known metaphorical concept, karaoke music, and move it to a new setting, PowerPoint.

2. Rules and Procedures

The rules control the actions that players can or cannot take. The procedures are ways in which the play will progress. The rules and procedures determine how the play will evolve and, in a sense, they are the glue that ties the play together. What distinguishes, for instance, the play design methods from mock-ups, sketches and prototypes are partly the layer of rules and procedures and partly the application of interactive feedback techniques to enforce these rules and procedures. Even in self-invented play situations, players instinctively begin to work towards more rules and procedures. In other words, they invent the rules as the play progresses. Playing on a swing together with a friend at the playground will sometimes generate rules such as: Who can put the

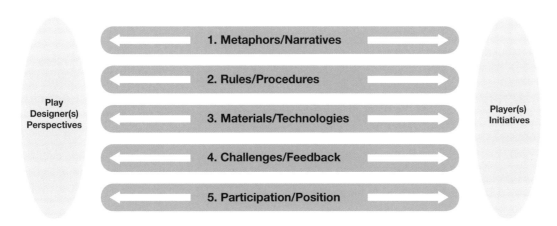

Figure 0.4: Five key ingredients in the boiling pot

most energy into this and swing the highest? When should we jump off the swing? Of course, the key question in most play design is what kinds of rules and procedures, if any, should be created before a specific play activity. For that reason, it is of crucial importance that we understand the flexibility of rules and procedures and see them as changing factors closely related to participation and the open-endedness of play (De Valk et al. 2013). Jess Rahbek (Ch. 3), in one of his play story examples, describes play around a sprinkler. At one point, it is established that the goal is to not get hit by the water and the rule is further elaborated to make this a harder challenge for the girls.

3. Materials and Technologies

The selection of materials to use in a given situation is important in play design. Materials such as foam, cardboard, fabric, felt and glass each have different advantages and disadvantages or constraints, or, in the words of Gibson, different affordances (Gibson 1966). Helle Marie Skovbjerg (Ch. 1) presents an example of the affordances of a doll with which a young girl is playing. In video games, a player loses the tangibility of the physical materials and the quality of thinking with his or her hands and body, but may, on the other hand, reach a higher degree of functionality or quick computational feedback. For that reason, it is of crucial importance to understand materials and technologies in close relation to context, orders of play, rules and procedures that appear during play and the changing role they may have during play. We can also think of space or spatial conditions as objects to play around with everything from chairs, tables, floor, walls or what constitutes outside environments.

Antonia Södergren (Ch. 7) shows how specific materials lead to various types of expressive interactions and imaginative constructions, as well as suggesting that pre-schoolers can exercise a high degree of imagination through build experiments. One element of many play activities is the exploration of what a specific object can deliver in terms of new meaning in the hands of specific players. The body can also become the material. For instance, Mathias Poulsen (Ch. 9) describes how dance is part of a festival called *CounterPlay* – not meant as a challenge to perform the best dance moves on the street but as a way to reach embodied deliberation.

4. Challenges and Feedback

Playground activities that are fun to begin with die out when they become too easy or boring because of repetition or lack of new play opportunities. Toys lose their charm if no new meanings are activated over time. Game designer Marc LeBlanc argues that two different factors provide the dramatic tension of a game. The first is uncertainty, 'the sense that the outcome of the contest is still unknown' (LeBlanc 2006). The second is inevitability, 'the sense that the contest is moving toward resolution' (ibid.). Jess Rahbek (Ch. 3) likewise highlights that play activities excel when a playful tension is established between the *orderly* and the *unruly*.

A significant feature of experiential-led activities such as play and games is the constant feedback gained from them. The moment this feedback ceases to change and we have already experienced it, the play activity will start to lose its attraction for us. Such instant feedback presents the opportunity to adjust or try something else, because on a practical level either something was missing to make the play work or players lacked the skill to overcome the challenge. Where does the feedback come from? It can come from any or all of the other ingredients or be reinforced by a play facilitator or computational feedback (algorithm). Objects such as the pinball game described by Sune Gudiksen (Ch. 10) can yield this feedback through random occurrences. An in-play metaphor or rule can shift our perception of the world or the specific situation at hand.

5. Participation and Position

This ingredient is related to the people in the play situations, their competencies, their experiences and the existing power relations between them. For several years, the term 'free play' has been used to describe the positions of the participants in play activities. Free play means that the players decide and create structure on their own, and cannot be instructed by somebody outside the 'magic circle' (Huizinga 1949). Conceptually, free play may not be the best way to describe participation in play. Play is never wholly 'free', but emerges out of a number of structures, relations and materials. We suggest the use of spontaneous play instead. Play design is first and foremost about designing for practices that allow participants to create possibilities for variations in the design. It is crucial to design for different play(er) roles for the participants to take and recreate, imagine and reimagine, in a close relationship with other participants. Helle Marie Skovbjerg (Ch. 1) describes the importance of the references of the players within the magic circle, which involves both repeating and exploring the limits of play practices. Tilde Bekker, Ben Schouten and Linda de Valk (Ch. 4) describe participation as taking positions by creating one's own structures through the concept of open-endedness.

The five key ingredients create a system in which a change in one ingredient will affect all the other ingredients and therefore the holistic play experience. Now we have the pot – the play space and the play spectrum. We have the salt (play designers) and sugar (players). We have five main ingredients, but we also need to know how to stir the pot.

The Stirring of the Play Pot

In some situations, a play facilitator can help mediate between intended design and perceived experience. Such a play facilitator may, depending on the setting or situation, be a trainer, teacher, change agent, play agent, play mediator or design facilitator. Someone involved in the development of new products, services or experiences may be called a *play design facilitator*, whereas someone who is involved when these are in use may be called a *play experience facilitator*.

The play design facilitator mediates, activates or helps participants reach imaginative states in the making of something new for others, whether this is a new product, service, activity or culture. The play experience facilitator supports a specific kind of experience of something that is already in place; for instance, the LEGO House experience centre has hired so-called play agents to assist visitors in going on a play journey in the house, making for fewer frustrations for the visitors and easier commissioning of a good play experience for the visitors.

The role of a play design facilitator or play experience facilitator is in general much the same. It is the act of *constraining* or *deconstraining* that differentiates them, acknowledging that participants are not uniform, but have different styles, preferences and needs on a specific day. Such a facilitator role can be seen as the elongated arm of the play design or play experience situation. The facilitator can intervene in an objective, sophisticated manner by the application of play feedback techniques, observing through trained eyes whether the play situation is troublesome and players need help or if it is too easy and therefore boring, and then may add rules or challenges. Furthermore, the facilitator may be the one who can identify and hold on to moments of surprise, which serve as the starting points for emergent patterns and imaginative states.

The facilitator sometimes elicits feedback by reinforcing uncertainty through new objectives, rules, etc., or by moving the play towards a close. Therefore, it can be either the materials that work as a boundary object or the facilitator or a combination of the two. In fact, the major difference between computer games and analogue play is that, in a computer game, the feedback is provided by computation (Juul 2003), while in analogue play design and play experience situations, the facilitator is a co-enabler of the feedback.

The facilitator can view the five key ingredients as a set of instruments that can be tuned during play. For instance, the facilitator can introduce metaphors or short stories, which would not be pre-determined but added as the play evolves. The facilitator may observe that a specific rule or procedure is not appropriate for a certain play situation, in which case the decision can be made, together with the participants, to omit this procedure. On the other hand, it may be that the participants have too many options, in which case the facilitator could suggest adding a rule or a procedure – that is, a constraint – that makes sense.

Adding or removing materials or technology elements during play is yet another way to either constrain or deconstrain a play design or experience. For instance, participants can be allowed to use whatever materials are within range, or the facilitator can restrict choices to only one type of material. Challenges can be adjusted to make them harder or easier. Participants can be regrouped or repositioned along the way, and the setting can be adapted or completely changed. All of these are in-play choices that a play

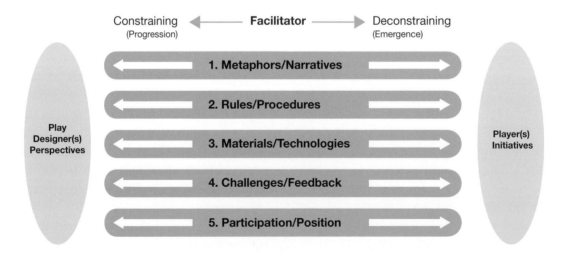

Figure 0.5: Play design facilitator & Play experience facilitator instrument line

design or play experience facilitator can take through careful observation of and attention to the players, guiding them towards a specific play situation or helping them let go of pre-made rules.

Three Key Play Flavours

Three major lines of thinking run through the history of play research, guiding specific ways of understanding the purpose and objectives of play.

Mood and atmosphere: a phenomenological way of understanding play in which mood and atmosphere are the main purpose.

Experience and surprise: a pragmatic way of understanding play that offers memorable or transformative experiences through series of surprises.

Construction with role play: a constructionistic way of comprehending the world through creating and using objects and props, and encouraging role play through the enactment with these.

Key Flavour – Mood and Atmosphere

Play design has the ability to create atmospheres and imaginative temporary worlds in which we let go of our 'normal' behaviour, seek new ways to create relationships, dive into specific interests and explore new avenues, without knowing what the activities might lead to.

When designing for play, we must recognize the importance of setting the scene for different meaningful relations and experiences, just as meanings differ if we are eating dinner or working at our desk.

The mood of play, this specific way of being in the world, can be understood through the concept of *Stimmung*, as set forth by the German philosopher Martin Heidegger (Heidegger 2005). According to Heidegger, a person is always in some kind of mood, even if his or her state of being suggests a lack of any mood. We never merely observe the world, because things only make sense from the place in which they are seen, in the contexts to which they belong and in terms of what has previously made sense to us and how we feel they should be included in an imminent future. In that sense, the production of meaning is not just something that we do from time to time but rather constitutes the way we are as human beings. Heidegger captures that point in his conceptualization of the human being as a *Dasein* – a being who is always already in place – *da* – and exists in a relationship with the world. To be in a play mood is thus one way in which an individual exists.

According to Heidegger, a mood is an indeterminate or undefined state that tells you something about your relationship with the world or how you are tuned in to the world and the people around you. Mood is an intermediated position where all is not said, although this does not mean that nothing is said. It is a way of being that is not confined to a specific meaning, but is ready for meaning to be articulated as something specific, whether or not this specification has happened yet.

The key point here is that mood cannot be understood as an inner psychological state of mind, as Csikszentmihalyi has stated (1989), coming from within, but rather something that arises in our engagement as beings in the world. Play designers are designing for this interrelation, creating opportunities for experiences of that relationship and for the mood to occur. As a consequence, the phenomenological is not only a one-person perspective but a social phenomenology, in which relationships are the main focus for exploring and designing for the creation of moods and atmosphere (Skovbjerg & Bekker 2018).

Helle Marie Skovbjerg (Ch. 1) further describes mood as a way of being in the world that can be operationalized as a concrete design practice, combining actual experiences of play with conceptualization of a new play design. Similarly, Mathias Poulsen (Ch. 9) underlines the importance of play as a way of being existentially together with other people in order to explore our shared lives. Likewise, Jesper Falck Legaard (Ch. 2) argues for the importance that play rest on intrinsic motivation as meaningfulness for participants might not occur otherwise – this is part of his categories of *motive orientations* (see Figure 2.3, Ch. 2). Also, Line Gad Christiansen (Ch. 8) argues for

the advantages for playing regularly - regardless of school, work or leisure setting – leads to a greater feeling of happiness and being able to on problems or turn them upside down.

Key Flavour – Experience and Surprise
Play is one of the principal immersive experiences: people engaged in play can be immersed so deeply in play activities that they fail to register what is happening around them. Toy, play and game design works to develop interaction patterns for such immersive experiences in the entertainment industry. However, in recent years, play- and game-based approaches have expanded to learning in general, creating beneficial experiential and learner-centred activities, where the learners take charge of the approach, how they want to learn and where they want to go. From her experiences in various educational settings, Line Gad Christiansen (Ch. 8) observes that there are still certain expectations related to instructivism that involve an expert standing, talking and showing prepared content in every last detail. Exercises, group work and small breaks are used to add variety. Now we also see play-based experiential activities being included more often.

At the heart of a memorable experience lie *curiosity* and *surprise*, which lead to perspective shifts and new actions, approaches, beliefs and routines. Play design can be used to propel participants out of habitual thinking and a status-quo understanding of the world into imaginative modes where they actively search for new meaning.

Surprise has often been noted as an element in strong new framings of problems and solutions, as identified by Schön's (Schön 1983; 1987) research, and, in accessing the worlds of the users, a large number of surprises can help inform play design methods (Gudiksen 2015; Feder 2020).

Several play design methods in this book suggest that educators let go of that kind of instructivistic mindset, relinquish some, if not all, of the control and, as Karen Feder (Ch. 5) argues, subject themselves to challenge. One of her methods, called *Internship as a child*, demonstrates that giving the control to the children is a fruitful way of understanding how they think and act. Similarly, Hanne Hede Jørgensen (Ch. 6) suggests the method of *Narrative inquiry* as a way of meeting the child as the unknown other, arguing that this gives access to a better understanding of the sense-making, presumptions and ideas the children may have.

Activating a series of surprises in play activities leads to what may be called kaleidoscopic patterns that offer a variety of meanings. Thus, we can aim for players to become *pattern breakers* in order to also become *pattern creators*.

Several researchers and experts in the overlapping fields of experience design and play design have attempted to create frameworks with the components needed to create memorable experiences, leading to some sort of transformation in the participants. For example, Korhonen et al. (2009) have developed the Playful Experiences (PLEX) framework, which categorizes playful experiences based on an analysis of theoretical work on pleasurable experiences, game experiences, emotions, elements of play and reasons why people play. The list of 22 experiences includes discovery, competition, fellowship, sympathy, fantasy and expression. Other examples of components from other authors are presented in Figure 6.

The list of such components and associated frameworks is unlikely to be fully exhaustive, although Jesper Falck Legaard (Ch. 2) approaches it both through a holistic framework of components and through descriptions of how to break it up so it becomes operational (see Figure 2.1, Ch. 2).

Key Flavour – Construction with Role Play

At the heart of active and concrete experiences lies a ludic constructionism agenda, where the type of action and experience is related to physical or digital constructs made by involved participants. Seymour Papert and Idit Harel (1991) introduced constructionism, distinguishing it from

The Overlap Between Experience Components and Play Components					
Experiences in General			Play Experiences		
Pine & Gilmore 1999/2007	Boswijk et al. 2007	Jantzen et al. 2010	Korhonen et a. 2009		Legaard 2019
Entertainment	High concentration	Interactivity	Captivation	Nurture	Investigation
Educational	All senses involved	Intimacy	Challenge	Relaxation	Construction
Escapist	Perception of time changed	Closeness	Competition	Sensation	Storytelling
Aesthetic	Touched emotionally	Authenticity	Completion	Simulation	Bodily activity
Authenticity	Uniqueness	Uniqueness	Control	Submission	Achievement
	The real thing	Inclusive	Cruelty	Subversion	Relatedness
	A process of during	Vibrant	Discovery	Suffering	Autonomy
		Learning	Eroticism	Sympathy	Pleasure
		Interesting	Exploration	Thrill	Virtue
		Relevance	Expression		Disruption
			Fantasy		Chance
			Fellowship		Humour
			Humour		Imagination

The list here does not show the complete frameworks from the authors. To understand how they define and interpret the listed terms and how they see the connections between each terms we suggest you directly to these sources.

Figure 0.6: Suggested components from various experience design and play design authors

constructivism. Constructivism assumes that understanding is gained through an active process of developing hypotheses and creating new forms of understanding through activity (Mayes & de Freitas 2013). In constructionism, the assumption is that learning 'happens especially felicitously in a context where the learner is consciously engaged in constructing a public entity'. Public entities are exemplified by sandcastles, dolls' houses, Lego building units and collections of cards. Constructionism has a focus on developing knowledge by working with concrete materials rather than abstract propositions. They further add (Papert & Harel 1991):

The weak claim is that it suits some people better than other modes of learning currently being used. The strong claim is that it is better for everyone than the prevalent 'instructionist' modes practised in schools. A variant of the strong claim is that this is the only framework that has been proposed that allows the full range of intellectual styles and preferences to each find a point of equilibrium.

For Papert and Harel, knowledge happens in the conversation with the material, which leads to self-directed learning. The materials help to bring out our inner feelings and ideas or, in the words of design specialist Jon Kolko (2010), ideas are 'externalized'. Ideas become tangible and can be shaped and sharpened, possibly through conversation with other people. It is also through the use of concrete, tangible materials that reflection-in-action frequently occurs, leading to new ways of approaching the situation at hand. Tangible materials access more senses in the play activity. Antonia Clasina Södergren (Ch. 7) adds that, through such constructions, a type of what she calls *expressive interactions*, participants also leave signs of the activities. This can be a way to remember what went on, picked up for subsequent activities or used for the generation of ideas.

The idea of theoreticians of childhood (for instance Jean Piaget and Lev Vygotsky) are partially revived in constructionism, but with an understanding that some of them are also valid for adulthood. This includes Piaget's (1969) research into the way children reason at various ages and Vygotsky's (1967) accounts of play in childhood. Material use helps especially in situations characterized by uncertainty and complexity and in which there is not only one answer. The objects are there to mediate communication and therefore function as a kind of stand-in for something else. Roos (2006) suggests that one can see these three-dimensional objects as tropes, which are figurative ways of speaking that challenge assumptions about status-quo understanding in participants and provoke the creation of new meanings.

The term trope is derived from the Greek word tropos, *turn, and this is very apt: by making the unfamiliar familiar or by making the familiar unfamiliar (Roos 2006).*

Such construction play includes various kinds of role play with the objects, items and props and often in collaborative play activities. All contributors mention such objects as a route to specific role plays. For instance, Line Gad Christiansen (Ch. 8) presents an example of a story in which objects such as dolls and teasets create role play, as well as negotiation between three children on how to proceed with the play activity. Hanne Hede Jørgensen (Ch. 6) tells of a narrative in which the children are curious about the sounds and affordances coming from metal barrels.

Karen Feder (Ch. 5) states that both designs or professional disciplines in which creating and making are core activities reflect the fact that children like to build and construct. This therefore becomes a common ground, a chance to develop ideas and learn together. The same is true for adults who have various professional work and cultural backgrounds, as illustrated by Sune Gudiksen (Ch. 10): here, building and making together are crucial ways of accessing imagination about the future and of letting go, at least for a while, status-quo understanding.

This is an essential part of what play design aims for: to create surprises through the use of three-dimensional objects and associated role play, and for the participants to extract new meaning from these often in collaborative manners.

Quick Take-Aways

We illustrated the mixture of key elements in play design using the metaphor of a boiling cooking pot.

The boiling pot is the play space boundary that is created within situational constraints. The contents of the pot are kept boiling through fluctuation between progression and emergent patterns, and in the tension between the orderly and the unruly.

A specific play design is developed by 'salt' (play designers) and 'sugar' (the players), while a play design facilitator or play experience facilitator stirs the pot. But the key ingredients are:

(1) metaphors and narratives that often turn into bigger story worlds, (2) rules and procedures that condition how the play unfolds, (3) the materials and technologies employed, (4) challenges and feedback, which contribute to the relevance of the play for the participants, and (5) participation and position, which challenge players to explore other angles, perspectives and positions.

Three flavours give the dish its distinctive taste: (1) mood and atmosphere, (2) experience and surprise, and (3) construction with role play.

Further Reading

Bateson, G. (2006). *A Theory of Play and Fantasy. The Game Design Reader. A Rules of Play Anthology*, 314-328.

Boswijk, A., Thijssen, T., & Peelen, E. (2007). *The Experience Economy: A New Perspective.* Pearson Education.

Buur, J., & Matthews, B. (2008). *Participatory Innovation.* International Journal of Innovation Management, 12(03), 255-273.

Caillois, R. (1961). *Man, Play, and Games.* University of Illinois Press.

Csikszentmihalyi M. & LeFevre J. (1989). *Optimal Experience in Work and Leisure.* Journal of Personality and Social Psychology 56(5):815-22.

De Valk, L., Bekker, T., & Eggen, B. (2013). *Leaving Room for Improvisation: towards a Design Approach for Open-ended Play.* In Proceedings of the 12th international conference on interaction design and children (pp. 92-101).

Ehn, P. (1993). *Scandinavian Design: On Participation and Skill. Participatory Design: Principles and Practices*, 41, 77.

Feder, K. (2020). *Exploring a Child-centred Design Approach – from Tools and Methods to Approach and Mindset.* Ph.D. Dissertation: Design school Kolding.

Gadamer, H-G. (2013). *Truth and Method.* Bloomsbury Publishing Plc. UK.

Gibson, J. J. (1966). *The Senses Considered as Perceptual Systems.* Praeger. Cornell University.

Gudiksen, S. K. (2014). *Game Feedback Techniques: Eliciting Big Surprises in Business Model Design. In Proceedings of DRS 2014*: Design's Big Debates: Design Research Society Biennial International Conference 16-19 June 2014, Umeå, Sweden (pp. 204-219). Umeå University.

Korhonen H., Montola M. and Arrasvuori J. (2009). *Understanding Playful Experiences through Digital Games.* Proc. DPPI '09, ACM (2009), 274-285.

Heidegger, M. (1938/1996). *Being and Time.* Oxford: Wiley-Blackwell.

Huizinga, J. (1949). *Homo Ludens: A Study of the Play Element in Culture* (3). Taylor & Francis.

Jantzen, C., Vetner, M., & Bouchet, J. (2010). *Oplevelsesdesign.* Samfundslitteratur.

Juul, J. (2003). Half-real: *Video Games between Real Rules and Fictional Worlds* (Doctoral dissertation, IT University of Copenhagen).

Kolb, D. A. (1984). *Experiential Learning: Experience as the Source of Learning and Development* (1). Prentice-Hall Englewood Cliffs, NJ.

Kolb, A. Y., & Kolb, D. A. (2010). *Learning to Play, Playing to Learn: A Case Study of a Ludic Learning Space.* Journal of Organizational Change Management, 23(1), 26-50.

Kolko, J. (2010). *Abductive Thinking and Sensemaking: The Drivers of Design Synthesis.* Design Issues, 26(1), 15-28.

Lakoff, G., & Johnson, M. (1980). *Metaphors we Live by.* University of Chicago press.

LeBlanc, M. (2006). *Tools for creating dramatic Game Dynamics. The Game Design Reader: A Rules of Play Anthology,* 438-459.

Legaard, J. F. (2019). *Nudges for Creativity: Integrating Elements from Play in Work Environments.* ISPIM Conference Proceedings, Florence, 2019.

Mainemelis, C., Altman, Y., Kolb, A. Y., & Kolb, D. A. (2010). *Learning to play, Playing to learn.* Journal of Organizational Change Management.

Mayes, T., & de Freitas, S. (2013). *Technology-enhanced Learning: The Role of Theory.* In Rethinking Pedagogy for a Digital Age (pp. 41-54). Routledge.

Piaget, J., & Inhelder, B. (1969). *The Psychology of the Child.* Basic Books.

Pine, B. J., Pine, J., & Gilmore, J. H. (1999). *The Experience Economy: Work is Theatre & every Business a Stage.* Harvard Business Press.

Playful learning research.(2020). *Playful Learning Research.* Retrieved at: https://playful-learning.dk

Roos, J. (2006). *Thinking from within: A Hands-on Strategy Practice.* Palgrave Macmillan.

Salen, K., Tekinba, K. S., & Zimmerman, E. (2004). *Rules of Play: Game Design Fundamentals.* MIT press.

Sanders, E. B. N., & Stappers, P. J. (2008). *Co-creation and the New Landscapes of Design.* Co-design, 4(1), 5-18.

Schön, D. A. (1983). *The reflective Practitioner: How Professionals Think in Action.* Basic books.

Schön, D. A. (1987). *Educating the Reflective Practitioner.* Jossey-Bass San Francisco.

Skovbjerg, H.M. (2018). *Counterplay 2017– 'this is Play!'* International Journal of Play. 7:1. 115-118.

Skovbjerg, H.M. & Bekker, T. (2018). The *Value of Play: Designing for Open-ended Play.* Designskolen Kolding. Inaugural Lectures.

Simonsen, J., & Robertson, T. (Eds.). (2012). *Routledge International Handbook of Participatory Design.* Routledge.

Soffel, J. (2016). *What are the 21st-century Skills every Student Needs.* In World Economic Forum (Vol. 10).

Sutton-Smith, B. (2001). *The Ambiguity of Play.* Harvard University Press.

Vygotsky, L. S. (1967). *Play and its Role in the Mental Development of the Child.* Journal of Russian and East European Psychology, 5(3), 6-18.

Zimmerman, E. (2015). *Manifesto for a Ludic Century. The Gameful World: Approaches, Issues, Applications,* 19-22.

Play Design Insight 1:
Designing for Play Moods in a Ludotorium

Helle Marie Skovbjerg

This chapter presents the play mood perspective as a theoretical framework for designing for play, and this framework is operationalised through the workshop format Ludotorium. In this view on play design, it is of crucial importance to have a language for what play is and qualify the designs in interesting ways. Designers can use the framework, just as pedagogues and teachers can use it with guidance from play researchers.

Introduction

The aims of this chapter are to provide readers with a play design framework, play as practices of mood (Skovbjerg 2020; Skovbjerg 2018), and show how this framework can be applied to a design workshop format named Ludotorium, which is used to explore play and develop play designs. In the exemplary cases presented here, play designers apply the play design framework as a catalyst for thinking of various play activities in the Ludotorium.

The play design framework can be used for different purposes. It can be employed as a starting point for gaining knowledge about what play is, typically in a design process known as research, with the aim of clarifying the aspects, dynamics and conceptualisations of play. It can also be used as a reflecting tool through which one can understand others' play designs. When designing play situations, the framework can be used to consider various design decisions, e.g. do we want quiet bodies and continuity in the play design, numerous materials as resources to play around with or social practices in open spaces that result in interactions? When using a prototype for play, the framework can be used as an evaluation tool (e.g. were all of the moods achieved or just some of them? Was the quality of play based on the number of moods achieved?). Overall, the framework can be used as a resource throughout the design process of research preparation, decision-making and evaluation.

In the context of play, mood is how you experience being in the world when you play. With inspiration from the German philosopher Martin Heidegger, mood comprises the special relationship that one has with the world. According to Heidegger, humans are always in some kind of mood, as we are never merely observing the world but constantly needing the world to be meaningful to us. In the mood of play, I am especially open-minded towards creating meaning; I am filled with hope for something meaningful to happen; and I bear a great trust in the people I am around. Mood is not something that I 'have' inside me – it is not an inner state of being. However, neither is it something external. Mood is understood as something that is created between people, materials, spaces and relations. It is this 'in-between' that we are designing for when we design play moods.

Ludotorium

A Ludotorium is a workshop format that frames open collaborations between different stakeholders who share a mutual interest in designing for play in a particular field, e.g. within education or organisations. A Ludotorium can be described as a lab, the aim of which is to ensure that there is a strong association between

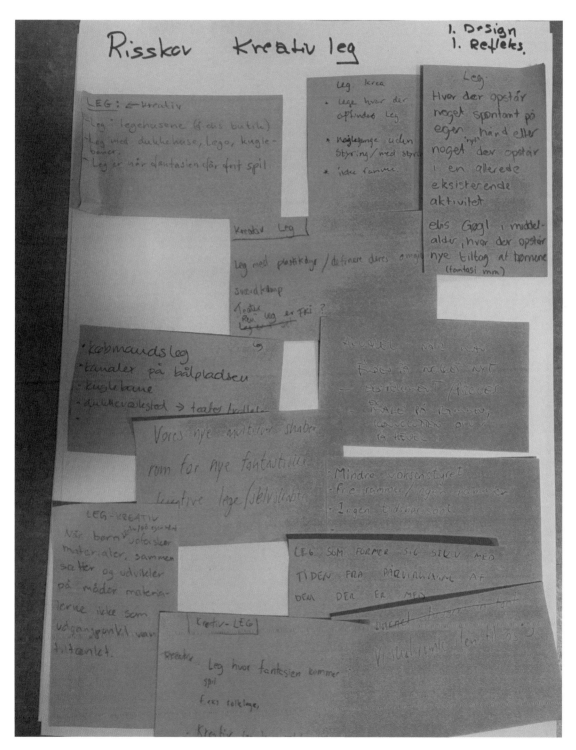

Figure 1.1: Pedagogues in 'Can I join in?' project

theories, practices-in-play and reflections on play. The aim involves making design decisions and experiencing how it feels to be in play. Inspired by design-based research (Amiel & Reeves 2008; Barab & Suire 2004; Brown 1992; Ejsing-Duun & Skovbjerg 2019), the Ludotorium is structured using a four-phased model. The first phase is the play order phase,

---

> **"**Play design is not a product that exists in a well-defined form – rather, it is something that is in constant development through what is done in the play activity**"**

---

where a play space is established; the second phase is the development phase, where the principles of play designs are created and structured; the third phase is play-in-practice, where play designs are tried out; and finally, the fourth phase is the reflection phase, where evaluations of and reflections on participants' experiences of each play design are explored.

Combining a theoretical framework for play and the Ludotorium play-in-practice is, to me, the foundation for the type of research practice and play design practice

that those working in this field must have. It is of crucial importance that the play designer's own experiences of cultivation and development in play-in-practice are evidenced. At the same time, developing and cultivating the language of those experiences comprise the foundation of play design creation.

Using a Play Framework for Play Designs: The Mood Perspective

In the mood perspective presented, play is primarily understood as a common way of living, being together and taking part in understanding the world around us. Play is about creating a way of living that is meaningful to you and the people you live with. For play designers, this means that their play design must follow the logic of play to ensure that it is meaningful. Understanding play as a life practice and a value in itself is not a new phenomenon. European philosophers have attempted to understand play as a life practice since the beginning of the last century. The German philosopher Friedrich Schiller's (2016) famous argument that only through play can an individual develop their full potential cemented play as a life practice.

An important aspect of the mood perspective is that it contrasts the understanding of play as a function of something else, such as learning, health, development or creativity. However, to view this as meaning that play in this perspective does not support all sorts of functions is incorrect. Rather, the play activity must primarily be seen as a way to describe how life can be lived in a meaningful way with others (Skovbjerg 2018; Skovbjerg 2013). For play designers, the consequences of looking at play in its own right are that the value of play is strongly related to life, meaning that participants' experiences of meaningful play designs are of crucial importance. The qualities of play design must, therefore, be strongly related to the participants' involvement in play activities (Skovbjerg 2018). However, while the experiences of being at play are crucial to what decisions the designer makes, the designer's own experiences of being at play can and must be actively used in the design process. In this sense, the consequence of this play perspective is that the designer's own play experiences and the cultivation of the designer's experiences and language for these experiences will be of crucial importance for the play mood being designed. Thus, in order to create play designs that successfully provide participants with experiences of being at play, play designers should be capable of playing themselves. They should also be able to apply the theoretical considerations of their play experiences to their design ideas and share these applications with their colleagues. In conclusion, the combination of theoretical consideration and play experiences will lead to stronger play designs.

Phase 1 – Play Order: Framing a Universe of Play Through a Ludotorium

When play occurs, movements, words, materials and relations can be perceived in a different way compared to when play is not occurring. The American researcher Gregory Bateson (1995) uses a concept of framing, initiating that 'this is play'. Bateson frames play activity as a distinct reality where what is meaningful and what is not might be understood differently. For example, when young children are taking part in roleplay, a tree can be framed as a castle for the king, a stick as a sword, and sentences such as 'I am the king of the world' are related to the narrative that they create. Thus, when designing for play, we must recognise the importance of setting the scene for meaningful relations that are not necessarily the same as eating dinner or working at our desks. The famous play researcher Johan Huizinga (2014) conceptualised this space of play as the magic circle – namely, a space that is different from everyday life. This creation of the universe of play is the first part of the framework of play as a mood practice.

In the first phase of the Ludotorium model – play order – we invite the participants into a safe space where we all create a universe where play has meaning. The participants can be adults or children. Both groups of participants can take part in the Ludotorium. In this first phase, we begin by 'setting' the play order with the participants by brainstorming which playful activities they appreciate most and why. Finally, we collect all the play qualities of the participants' stories to ensure that the meanings and values help set the stage for play.

Case 1 – The Play Order Phase

In the research project, 'Can I join in?', we worked with social educators in two Danish schools as the co-designers of play designs. We held two meetings to create the play order, where we uncovered the play qualities, as described in the first phase of the Ludotorium. We used design tools to support play coverage and brainstorming. The social educator Troels said that he used the first phase of the Ludotorium to immerse himself in the play order and that it was absolutely crucial for him to create a space where the play has value and where he, in collaboration with researchers and colleagues, can create and share this play order.

Phase 2 – LAB: Play Practices as Design Principles

The second phase of the Ludotorium is related to coming up with design ideas formulated from design principles based on the understanding of practice in the mood perspective. In addition, to play in the mood perspective, the play's action is central to the mood perspective. This section explores the actions that can be conducted in play that are conceptualised as play practice (Skovbjerg 2018; Skovbjerg 2013).

Play practice relates to all the 'doings' of play – namely, all the behaviours that one shows when playing, such as physical and mental activities, the use of ob-

Play practice	SLIDING	SHIFTING	DISPLAYING	EXCEEDING
Qualities	Following the practice Not changing Non-stop continuity Adjusting Repetitive rhythm Discrete and introvert	Movement Physical Motion Change in direction, heights and speed.	Showing yourself off Relation between me and the audience Exhibition Public performance	Constantly changing Exceeding of practices Contrast Testing Morbid Conflicting practices

Figure 1.2: Play practices as design principles

jects and toys, ways of relating to others and bodily movements and actions. These play practices create a meaningful universe around the play activity and, as the American play researcher Corsaros claims, players understand play culture through repetition but also occasionally create variations by interpreting what they do. Thus, they innovate play practices through their participation in said practices. The play practices involve repeating the actions and interpreting the actions and, as a consequence, play design is not a product that exists in a well-defined form – rather, it is something that is in constant development through what is done in the play activity.

The mood perspective consists of four archetypes of play practices. The first play practice is SLIDING. Here, the actions are characterised by a strong rate of repetition. They are consistent and uninterrupted, and the player should not change them too much but rather follow that repetition. The following is an example of SLIDING in play: Anna is a four-year-old girl who has been playing with her doll for four hours in the family living room. Anna takes the doll, puts the bottle in the doll's mouth, puts the doll in the cradle and rocks the doll. Following this sequence, Anna takes the doll, puts the bottle in the doll's mouth, etc.

SHIFTING is the second archetype of play practice. SHIFTING actions occur in play designs where participants use their entire body and move it in different directions and elevations. We often see this practice in large play designs such as trampolines, roller coasters and swings. For an example of SHIFTING, consider someone who is executing continuously high jumps on a trampoline, and then suddenly changes their body's direction and height.

DISPLAYING, the third archetype of play practice, involves an individual performing actions to someone who then judges these actions, like an audience for the play practices. When the actions are performed, there is an expectation that there will be continuous development of what is shown. Examples of these play actions in play designs include circus play and X factor play, where the children repeat some play actions linked to the relevant play design, while also putting personal touches on the expression and extravagance of their act.

EXCEEDING is the fourth archetype of play practice and is characterised by constantly looking to change, mock, tease or humour an individual with the actions that were previously established. The following is an example of this type of play action: Maja and Sarah are playing with puppets. Rather than exhibiting care and tenderness with the puppets, they make them appear angry and perform violent actions. The girls' play practices transcend the cultural codes of puppetry, and they indulge in mania.

Example: Case 2 – The LAB Phase

When we conducted a Ludotorium with the Danish Play Think Tank, we divided the fifty participants into groups of four. One group chose to work with the design principles from the SHIFTING and EXCEEDING play practices. Based on these design principles and their own experiences with full-body play designs, they began to make design decisions. This case is a good example of the argument that all play design is a combination of knowledge and theory about play and experiences with play. The group eventually created the following play design: All the participants are on the floor. One player walks to three people. The player has to run around the first person, the second person has to crawl under the player's legs, and the player has to jump over the last person. The group referred to this play design as over–under–around.

Phase 3 – Play-in-Practice: Play Moods in Play

In play-in-practice, the third phase of the Ludotorium, the play designs are developed based on the design principles of the second phase. The play designs are 'tested', meaning that in the third phase, we determine whether the actions we have designed lead to what we hoped for. For example, toy designers test and exhibit toy designs, and then all the participants play with the presented toy designs. This means that we will play with a large number of playful activities that are based on different compositions of the design principles from the mood perspective (Skovbjerg 2020; Skovbjerg 2018).

In the mood perspective, moods are closely linked to play practices, meaning that we can achieve moods through actions. In concrete terms, it is when

Play practice	SLIDING	SHIFTING	DISPLAYING	EXCEEDING
Play moods	Devotion	Excited	Tense	Euphoric
Qualities	Being absorbed Sense of following the practice Non-stop continuity	Affected body Butterflies in stomach Movement Physicality and enthusiasm	Tension in attention Extrovert, showing and bling	Feeling of manic Bizarre Extrovert, wild and expressive

Figure 1.3: Play practices and play moods as design principles

Figure 1.4: Play jam ideation and testing

we begin to practice the actions that we achieve play mood. Similar to actions, moods are divided into four archetypes that are associated with certain archetypes of the actions. Specifically, this means that when I perform SLIDING practices, which are characterised by strong repetitions, consistency in execution, calm bodies and predictability, I achieve devotion, which is the first mood. Devotion as a play mood is characterised by being in a state of flow, tuning in and experiencing non-stop movement. It feels effortless and absorbing, and the experience is discreet and often introverted.

The second mood – excitement – is linked to the practice of SHIFTING. In this playing mood, the body and senses are affected and there is an intense experience of being present, with the body going unexpected places. The full-body movement is important in this playing mood.

The third play mood is tension, which is related to the play practice of DISPLAYING. This play mood is characterised by the fact that one is prepared to perform and is aware that others are also performing. The mood is influenced by openness and the expectation of change, and there is a readiness for other people's interpretations in terms of how DISPLAYING is practised.

The last play mood is euphoria and is related to EXCEEDING. The mood is characterised by an intense expectation that wild or silly things will happen, and one is ready for other people's silliness. There is an expectation that new and crazy ideas will be discovered in order to remain in the euphoric mood of play. However, if the mood is not feeding off other crazy ideas, it will end. The following is an example of this mood: You are at a party with your friends, and someone tells a joke. Then, others follow up on the joke by telling another joke that is even crazier than the first.

If we return to the Ludotorium one of the groups had designed a small play activity (over-under-around), and in this phase, we tryed out the play together. This meant that we could test whether the mood that the actions should create actually occurred. I can reveal that the moods were both marked by excitement and euphoria, especially because those who tried to do something different at the same time (through the design principle of contradictory actions) ended up having a bizarre experience.

Phase 4 – Reflection on Experiences of Play-in-practice and Play Design Principles

In the reflection phase – the fourth phase of the Ludotorium – we reflect on the experiences that the third phase resulted in. We return to our design principles,

Play Practice	SLIDING	SHIFTING	DISPLAYING	EXCEEDING
Play Moods	devotion	excited	tense	euphoric

Figure 1.5: Overview of connection between play moods and play practices

which we selected in the second phase, and examine whether they should be refined based on the experiences we have had, just as we determine whether other play design principles also emerged during our experiences with the game. Overall, the goal of this phase is to sharpen our insights into the play as we nuance the principles to ensure that play leads to the desired mood quality.

During the try out of the play over-under-around, the participants reflected on their experiences. They found that the exact connection between the play design principles from SHIFTING and EXCEEDING worked well because they intensified each other in the testing of the play. This meant that the design, the design principles and the overall test made it easier for the participants to determine which combinations of design principles would create a particular mood.

Reflecting and sharing on the mood experiences that the participants had resulted in more of a focus on design decisions. A reflection that arose from this process was the question of whether we always design for one mood, thus enabling other moods to happen, or whether we always design for co-existing moods. Based on a number of empirical examples and the reflections within this case, the answer might be that we do both. However, the important point is that when designing for play, several moods must be possible. Otherwise, the play activity becomes irrelevant. The way in which play unfolds means that it will always seek to explore more than one mood in our designs.

Quick Take-Aways

This chapter has presented a theoretical framework for play and shown how it can be used in the Ludotorium design workshop format. The four phases of the Ludotorium, in combination with the theoretical framework used to understand play, create possibilities for play designers to structure their design process between thinking and doing and between trying out and reflecting on it. It also allows them to explore how their own experiences and assumptions of qualities of play can influence their design intentions and decisions. On one hand, it is of crucial importance that play designers design by combining their own experiences with play-in-practice. On the other hand, conceptualising that experience ensures that it is possible to share arguments for specific design intentions and design decisions. Some of the consequences of this perspective and approach are that play design must always be understood in terms of the context in which it is being developed, and here, the designer's own experiences must be reflected within these contexts. It is crucial for the designer to find strategies for how reflections of these terms can be seen and shared with colleagues and collaborators. The Ludotorium approach presents the possibility of structuring that reflection.

Further Reading

Amiel, T. & Reeves, T. C. (2008). Design-based Research and educational Technology: Rethinking Technology and the Research Agenda. *Educational Technology & Society*, 11(4), 29–40.

Barab, S. A. & Suire, D. (2004). Design-based Research: Putting a Stake in the Ground. *The Journal of the Learning Sciences*, 13(1). 1-14.

Bateson, G. (1955/2001). The Theory of Play and Fantasy. In G. Bateson (Ed.), *Steps to an Ecology of Mind: Collected Essays in Anthropology, Psychiatry, Evolution, and Epistemology* (pp. 75–80). Chicago: University of Chicago Press.

Brown, A. (1992). Design Experiments: Theoretical and Methodological Challenges in Creating Complex Interventions in Classroom Settings. *The Journal of the Learning Sciences*, 2(2), 141–178.

Ejsing-Duun, S. & Skovbjerg, H. M. (2019). Design as a Mode of Inquiry in Design Pedagogy and Design Thinking. *International Journal of Art and Design Education*, 38, 445–460.

Huizinga, J. (2014). *Homo Ludens: A Study of the Play-element in Culture.* UK: Martino Fine Books.

Schiller, F. (2016). *On the aesthetic Education of Man.* London: Penguin Books.

Skovbjerg, H. M. (2020). *About Play.* Copenhagen: Timeless Publishing.

Skovbjerg, H. M. (2018). *The Value of Play.* Design School Kolding. Inaugural Lecture.

Skovbjerg, H. M. (2013). Play Practices and Play Moods. *International Journal of Play*, 2(2), 76-86.

Play Design Insight 2:

Designing for Play(ful) Experiences

Jesper Falck Legaard

The following chapter describes an operational approach to understanding and designing for meaningful play experiences, using a framework entitled 'Play Blueprint'. It is relevant for those who develop products specifically for play activities or for those who see a value in the qualities of play as something that can enhance creativity and engagement in other settings, for instance, at a workplace.

Introduction

There is an extensive body of play research providing insights into play as a concept and ways of understanding play experiences and how they occur. But there is a lack of frameworks or theories at a more operational level that can guide those interested in designing for particular play experiences at a hands-on level. The following chapter describes a framework – the Play Blueprint – developed for that purpose: to provide an operational approach to designing for play experiences.

Play experiences are by nature coherent and experienced as unity in line with the phenomenological view of a meaningful experience (Gadamer 1975), but the Play Blueprint allows us to conceptually divide the play experience into components in order to make the experiences easier to define and design for, understanding a situation from what the participants experience in it. No matter if you are designing playground equipment and need to understand the play value, if you are designing a toy car and want to explore the possible play situations, or even if you are designing a new office space and want to infuse playful and creative behaviour into the employees, the blueprint will be a useful tool to guide the design towards meaningful play experiences.

It is called a blueprint because it is intended to be used as a scaffold for understanding particular play experiences through explicating its components; it can be used both analytically for examining and understanding current play experiences, but also as an approach for idea generation for new types of play experiences. The Play Blueprint is not temporal, meaning that it defines instances of the play experience, and as such, it can look differently at different stages of the play experience.

"*Play Blueprint allows us to conceptually divide the play experience into components in order to make the experiences easier to define and design for*"

The basis for the development of the blueprint is both play theory (e.g. Hedegaard 2016; Huizinga 1955; Sutton-Smith 1997) and studies of experiences and behaviour (e.g. Csikszentmihalyi 1990; Desmet & Pohlmeyer 2013; Fogg 2009; Jensen 2014; Ryan and Deci 2000). The blueprint was further developed through empirical studies of play experiences and has been applied to and refined via a diverse range of play-related design projects.

Although the blueprint defines components that we look for in the experiences,

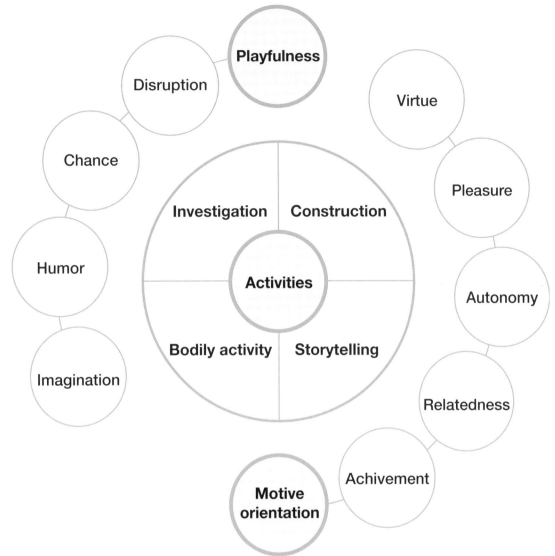

Figure 2.1: Play blueprint

the approach aims to be as free as possible from conceptual presuppositions. It is a way of observing and characterising the experience as we see it and does not propose something that should be present in the experience or seek to explain it through a particular lens. Therefore,

it should not be considered a recipe for meaningful experiences. A play experience does not necessarily become better or more meaningful the more components it contains – rather, there must be a balance that is coherent within the experience, i.e. as a unity of meaning.

Defining Play Experiences

The focus on experiences – and not just on the concept 'play' – emphasises the importance of individual experiences of people as conscious human beings. For this reason, the Play Blueprint takes the perspective of those having the experience but is a tool for those designing for the experience.

This representation can be a toy, an interactive garment, an app, a board game, or the design of physical work environment, underlining that the blueprint is applicable to almost all situations in which developers aim to enable a play(ful) experience by design. This can both be in relation to play experiences (playing purely for the sake of play) and playful experiences (for instance aiming to increase playfulness as a method for enhancing creativity at a workplace).

In short, the blueprint is intended as a tool for those designing artefacts for play(ful) experiences, aiding them in exploring the experience from the players' perspective.

Defining play experiences is, in this case, done with a focus on three main categories: Activities, Motive orientation and Playfulness.

Play is an intrinsically motivated experience evolving around explorative activities, triggering a sense of playfulness in those who participate.

These categories essentially refer to the questions of 'what?' (activities – what are the people playing actually doing?), 'why?' (motive orientation – why do the people playing want to engage in this play activity?) and a 'how?' (playfulness – what is the modus of the players in the activity? How does the way people engage with the artefact become playful?) To fully understand what those categories contain, they have been divided into specific components as illustrated in Figure 2.1.

Play Activities

Play experiences are centred around activities, i.e. describing 'what' the persons playing are doing. Riding a bicycle around a cycle track, for instance, can be a play activity. They are described as activities rather than distinctive 'types' of play because a play experience is rarely restricted to one unique type, but rather a combination of activities. Constructing with bricks, for instance, is rarely only about construction but typically includes an equally important element of storytelling, for instance, building a castle for a king and his queen. There are four main play activities, described in Figure 2.2.

Investigation
Small children often do simple, basic investigations of the characteristics of different objects, but for larger children and adults it becomes more complex, typically focusing on the relation between things

Figure 2.2: Play blueprint – activities

or investigating relations between oneself and others. Investigation aims at examining an object or relation, narrowing in on a specific understanding of it.

Construction

Construction refers to an activity where those playing manipulate their environment to create things. A typical example of a construction activity is building with bricks. But all 'hands-on' explorations through combining and manipulating materials to construct something new are considered constructive activities.

Storytelling

Through storytelling, the player develops a narrative that is inherent in most play activities. The term 'storytelling' is used to underline the active development of the story, for instance, created through roleplaying or playing with dolls or action figures.

Bodily Activity

Bodily activities range from being physically intense, such as running or fighting, to calmer sensorial experiences, such as using a slide or a swing. These activities challenge and stimulate the senses and one's gross motor skills.

Motive Orientations

To understand and design for meaningful play experiences, it is of high importance to understand what makes the experience valuable for the person(s) playing, i.e. understanding 'why' they would be motivated to play. The blueprint addresses five motive orientations which can be considered the intentions of the player that the play activity is directed at. These intentions (although not always knowingly) are the player's motivation for engaging in a play activity. For this motivation to be inherent in the play experience (which is crucial for it to be a play experience), the motivation needs to come from something that complies with the underlying desire of the person playing. The play activity does not become meaningful and engaging if it is directed at something that we are generally opposed to because that does not lead to intrinsic motivation. There are five motive orientations, described in Figure 2.3.

Achievement

Achievement links to 'competence', comparative to what Deterding (2013) described as mastery. In game design (as in

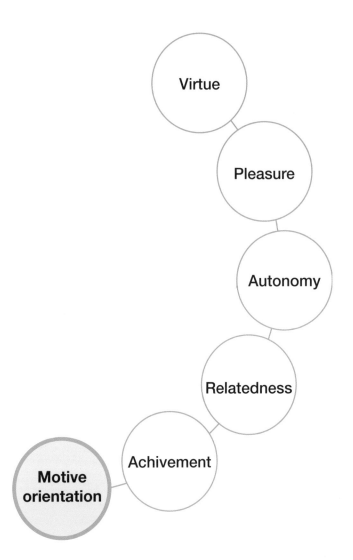

Figure 2.3: Play blueprint – motive orientations

Relatedness

Social relations are often an important part of our experiences. In play, we can, for instance, be motivated by the possibility of teasing the other players, to be acknowledged, in some cases even admired, or the collaboration between players. Relatedness addresses all these factors – collaboration, teasing, challenging, showing off and other aspects of playing that are defined by the relations to other players or spectators.

Autonomy

Autonomy links to the characteristics of play experiences as being free and explorative. We express autonomy when we do things in our own way, take responsibility, and make our own decisions. In that sense, play experiences crave the freedom of the player to be explorative in order for the player to find their own path through the experience.

Pleasure

The concept of pleasure can, for instance, be the aesthetic pleasure of a product considered beautiful, or it could be the use of haptic feedback, where the player feels a sensation when they do something specific. These visual or sensorial pleasures can enhance positive engagement in a play experience. Other examples are magnets that 'magically' snap into place, or the feeling when a game of solitaire is completed. Humans generally appreciate the systematics of things that fit together in an orderly

play), the player needs interesting challenges that comply with and build upon his skill level. They must be both difficult (prone to lead to failures) but also achievable at some point (Csikszentmihalyi 1990).

The word achievement is used because it makes it active, that something must be achieved. It thereby gives the building of 'competence' an inherent purpose.

fashion or 'make sense', although there has to be a balance between the chaos and the order. We need the chaos to make the order interesting and fulfilling.

Virtue

Virtue can, for instance, be expressed by doing certain things in order to, for instance, do something good for the environment. But it can also be helping one's parents by doing the dishes. For a child, virtue is often related to having a meaningful role in the family and taking part in the responsibilities within the family. But virtue in play is slightly different in that it refers to the imaginative space of the play activity. Being a white knight that saves a princess from a dragon, for instance.

Playfulness

The third category focuses on playfulness, considered as an 'attitude of play' and further as 'a projection of characteristics into an activity' which, in cases where the activity is not free play, lacks the autotelic nature that is characteristic of play experiences. Playfulness, in that case, can preserve the purpose of the activity it is applied to, relating it also to the concept of gamification.

Playfulness underlies the assumption that 'joy of use' is not necessarily the same as (and in some cases, even opposite of) 'ease of use', suggesting a counterpoint to usability. Based on empirical studies

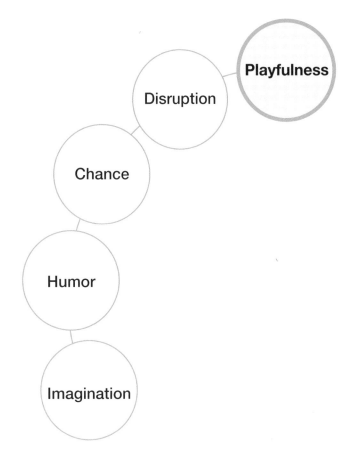

Figure 2.4: Four concepts for playfulness

of play experiences, four concepts for playfulness were identified. These are described below.

Disruption

Disruption builds on the play paradox, balancing between what is allowed and what is not. This is the danger and boldness of play that acts on the verge of destruction, risking that the play experience will come to a sudden end.

If a child uses a hammer to play the piano, for instance. It becomes playful because he is doing something unintended (and something he knows he probably shouldn't do) to see what the effect will be. This action also supports his feeling of autonomy, because he is disrupting the play experience in his own way, exploring the consequences of doing something unintended.

Chance

Play experiences defined as explorations suggest inherent opportunities to make new discoveries, finding something unexpected or making new connections. This is ignited by a degree of randomness, i.e. the potential for something unexpected to happen. Play has an intrinsic insecurity about where it is taking us and what is going to happen in which play links to the concept of emergence. When we play, something that we could not have foreseen emerges. This uncertainty – positively described as serendipity – can force us to experience something with playful astonishment.

Humour

Humour is typically something that originates from our social relations, but we can also try to design objects that afford humorous situations to occur or that express humour through their design. Such objects often build on quirkiness, exaggeration, surprise, humanisation and imagination, for instance, making things that are out of scale or adding quirky personalities to inanimate objects.

Imagination

Play experiences typically unfold in a realm of their own, typically in a middle ground between reality and imagination. The creation of such a meta-reality requires the element of imagination. In most cases, imagination requires a starting point – for instance, a castle in which a knight can live if the players are children – or simply the use of roles or metaphors if the players are adults. When grown-ups, for instance, play soccer and a player calls himself Messi, he takes on a role that adds to the playfulness of the experience.

"By using the blueprint, we can add value, meaning, engagement and creativity to most situations, designing a world for the playful human being."

The Blueprint as a Design Tool

Designing is basically an iterative process that switches continually between creative exploration and analytic decision-making. Using the blueprint as a tool in the design process can guide the development towards a meaningful play ex-

Figure 2.5: Students conceptualising pl
designs following use of the bluepri

perience, both by aiding discovery of the right/useful aspects and by supporting creative ideation.

Besides being used for developing products for play, it can be used in relation to situations other than 'typical' play situations, e.g. for developing more creative work environments. For such situations the Play Blueprint activate important insights for a workspace since play and playfulness are often linked to motivation, creativity and a sense of wellbeing.

How to use the blueprint depends on the situation and the intended outcome, as described in the following examples.

Designing for
New Play Experiences

The blueprint is applicable as a tool to drive creativity towards new ideas for play experiences. It can be used simply to point ideation in different directions, for instance asking 'what would happen if we tried to add more humour to this experience', or 'how could we make this activity more social', focusing on two of the described elements in the blueprint.

For ideation purposes, we often use a template based on the Play Blueprint. Starting with a 'How might we…?' question, for instance, 'How might we develop a swing for young children?', participants are asked to focus on one component of the blueprint at a time. The particular component to focus on is decided randomly (e.g. by spinning a bottle). If the bottle points to [ACHIEVEMENT], for instance, they would create ideas for how the swing could enable a sense of achievement, e.g. showing your max height using LED lighting or developing music when you hit and sustain a certain rhythm in the swing activity.

The participants will focus on only that component for a couple of minutes, then spin the bottle again to get a new direction (for instance: 'Now add [IMAGINATION] to your current play-ideas'.)

Say that, for instance, you are working on a playground developing a new structure for children to climb on. In the concepts you already developed, there are a lot of physical play possibilities.

Doing this ideation exercise might then challenge you to 'add [RELATEDNESS]' to your concept, which could lead to ideas for developing the concept in ways that allow children to play together, further challenging their balance and coordination through the collaboration. You could also be asked to add [IMAGINATION], which could lead you to design it as a spaceship the children have to enter and climb around in.

In this way, using the blueprint for idea generation and development can guide you to take your concept in new directions, leading to more fun and engaging play experiences.

To also make the ideation activity playful (as any ideation process should be), we also designed the activity using the blueprint, for instance, including the bottle as something that adds bodily activity and randomness to the ideation process. Furthermore, we added disruptive activities by including a dice roll. We set up particular rules for the roll of the dice, stating that if a participant throws the dice and lands on 1, he has to switch his best idea with the worst idea from one of the other participants. If it was a 6, he would have to draw sketches for new ideas upside down. If it was 2–5, he got to spin the bottle and continue with a new component to focus on.

Quick Advice

The described way of doing ideation is both fun and engaging, while providing an outcome of a wide range of different ideas. The random nature of such a set-up however also reduces the meticulousness of the outcome, which means that it can be a good idea to ensure that all other aspects are explored more deliberately, and not just working on those that were picked out randomly.

Developing Playful Work Environments

Some of the biggest challenges for knowledge-based companies in the digital age is to maintain a high level of creativity and innovation and to increase the engagement and wellbeing of the employees. An approach to solve this challenge is to develop a physical workplace that can 'nudge' employees towards certain behavioural patterns, which also has a large impact on the culture and mindset of the employees (Legaard 2019).

As an example, we did a project with a Danish company who wished to infuse the work environment with playfulness, intending to make the environment more comfortable while also increasing the level of creativity. In this case, we used the Play Blueprint as a tool for inspiring new ideas for meeting rooms and workspace interiors, for example, primarily focusing on the concepts of imagination and relatedness.

Fire in the hole!

If you were to enter a pirate ship, it would seem a natural (and, thus, accepted) behaviour to take on the role of a pirate. But it might seem strange if your financial adviser started acting as a pirate while you were sitting at his desk discussing your pension plans.

In this case, we created ideas for a new meeting room in the middle of a large open space, which was designed to look like a pirate ship. This was a way to draw upon qualities from roleplaying without actually playing. A playful environment like this can also aid to switch the awareness of 'me, my boss and my colleagues' to 'our team, our boat and our mission', which tends to elevate team spirit, engagement and collaboration.

Even in a 'serious' context, entering a pirate ship, for example, to define the vision and strategy of the company can be quite effective as a way to open up the discussion about how to 'set sails' and 'man the ship' in a more creative and engaging way than sitting around a table.

What makes people engage (or not) in play(ful) activities? When designing for play experiences it is important to remember that the inherent requirement for personal engagement in an experience in order to play can push the bound-

aries of those playing towards the limits of their comfort zones. This is also the reason why we typically learn much more about each other by playing together than by just talking to each other.

Those playing must feel safe and secure, not only in the sense of physical security (not being harmed) but also that the actions they must do in the play situation do not push them beyond their comfort zone. Playful physical environments that are poorly designed can become too 'silly', far-fetched, uncomfortable or inefficient to be used. On the other hand, a playful physical environment that is well designed can foster creativity, support social relations and provide a safe space for playful behaviour to unfold. So, there is an important balance between feeling safe and feeling intrigued or challenged by the experience, which can also be addressed using the Play Blueprint. Exploring the possibilities within the different concepts – for instance, finding the right level of imagination in the design – could be an example of a focus area. Would a pirate ship be too silly for your workplace (in which case people would not feel safe participating) or is it just strange enough to awake curiosity, spark creativity and add some humour?

In terms of transforming the culture in a workplace, the focus must be on designing an environment that nudges people to change the way they behave and relate to each other and does so by incorporating affordances in the design that remind them to keep behaving in this way, hereby enhancing the desired habits. This is an important aspect of creating lasting engagement.

Now it's your turn to play. The examples above illustrate how the Play Blueprint can be used as a tool to understand and design for play experiences in many different contexts. By using the blueprint, we can add value, meaning, engagement and creativity to most situations, designing a world for the playful human being.

Now it is your turn to try it out to better understand the human perspective of your organisation, to disrupt your usual design process, or just to get a better sense of what it means to have a meaningful (play) experience. In other words, just play around with it and see where it takes you.

Quick Take-Aways

Pushing the intended play experiences in different directions during the design process can often lead to more meaningful and engaging designs for play.

Seeing play not only as the outcome but also as part of the design process can increase the creative exploration during the process, which typically also leads to stronger designs.

Play and work are not opposites. A playful atmosphere at the workplace can improve the creativity, heighten the energy level and increase the engagement and wellbeing of the employees.

Using a framework – such as the Play Blueprint – is a good way to unfold possible paths for understanding and exploration. But it is not a recipe. It should be explored, 'played around with' and adapted to fit each particular situation or challenge.

Further Reading

To read more about Play Blueprint and find available Templates go to www. Playdesign.dk

Csikszentmihalyi, M. (1990). *Flow: The Psychology of Optimal Experience.* New York: Harper and Row.

Desmet, P. M. A. & Pohlmeyer, A. E. (2013). Positive Design: An Introduction to Design for Subjective Wellbeing. *International Journal of Design* 7(3): 5–19.

Deterding, S. (2013). Gameful Design for Learning. *T + D,* 67(7), 60-63.

Fogg, B. J. (2009). A Behaviour Model for Persuasive Design. *Proceedings of the 4th International Conference on Persuasive Technology,* April 26-29, 2009, Claremont, California, USA.

Gadamer, H. G. (1975). *Truth and Method.* Seabury Press.

Hedegaard, M. (2016). Imagination and Emotion in Children's Play: A Cultural-historical Approach. *International Research in Early Childhood Education* 59 Vol. 7, No. 2, 59-74.

Huizinga, J. (1955). *Homo Ludens: A Study of the Play-element in Culture.* Boston: Beacon Press.

Legaard, J. F. (2019). Nudges for Creativity: Integrating Elements from Play in Work Environments. *ISPIM Conference Proceedings,* Florence, 2019.

Ryan, R. M. & Deci, E. L. (2000). Self-determination Theory and the Facilitation of Intrinsic Motivation, Social Development and Well-being. *American Psychologist,* 55, 68-78.

Sutton-Smith, B. (1997). *The Ambiguity of Play.* Cambridge, MA: Harvard University Press.

Acknowledgement

I would like to thank all the students and companies who have contributed to the development of the blueprint through participating with engagement and enthusiasm in the exercises and activities I have put them through.

Play Design Insight 3:
Designing for Playful Tension

Jess Rahbek

This chapter introduces the Playful Tension perspective as a way of conceptualising new play designs. The perspective was developed in collaboration with the play design team at LEGO House – an exhibition and play experience center – where it is used in concept development and evaluation of their play designs.

Introduction

As a play designer, you are in the business of providing a good play experience for someone. In doing so, the basic question you need to ask yourself is: How can I make good play happen? This chapter will present a model that addresses the underlying nature of a play experience and how different design decisions can help initiate and sustain play.

It goes without saying that people are perfectly able to play without the aid of play designers. We can play with a rock or dream up our own stories and characters, but a well-designed toy, game, playground, etc. arguably makes it a lot easier for us to get started and sustain the play experience and grow it into something great. So, what exactly is it that great play designers do that makes our own play come easy? The Playful Tension perspective proposes that play designers do so by designing for experiences that create a tension between the orderly and unruly aspects of the experience.

Foundation of the Playful Tension Perspective

The Playful Tension perspective was developed as part of a collaborative research project between Design School Kolding, LEGO House and the LEGO Foundation with the aim of investigating the relationship between the practice of play design and the quality of the play experience.

The Playful Tension perspective begins with the assumption that we cannot design for play without knowing what play is. Now, we all have our own personal experiences and knowledge of play but if we are to conduct play design as a professional and reflective design discipline, then we cannot rely solely on gut-feel and tacit knowledge when making design decisions. In a professional environment such as LEGO House, it is crucial that team members have a shared understanding and language of play in order to productively discuss their design goals, intentions and decisions.

The problem of getting to a shared understanding of play is that the theoretical body of literature devoted to defining play and its function is relatively large and diverse as it spans centuries of studies across the fields of philosophy, psychology, sociology and biology. With play designers working in agile and iterative design processes with tight deadlines and budget concerns, we cannot expect them to read everything from Plato to the latest neuroscience studies before they start doing anything. With this challenge in mind, the Playful Tension perspective was developed from identifying the paradoxical double-sided nature of play as the single most common and consistent concept of play across the sampled academic literature. As such, the Playful Tension perspective was created by sampling play theories into a meta-theory by recog-

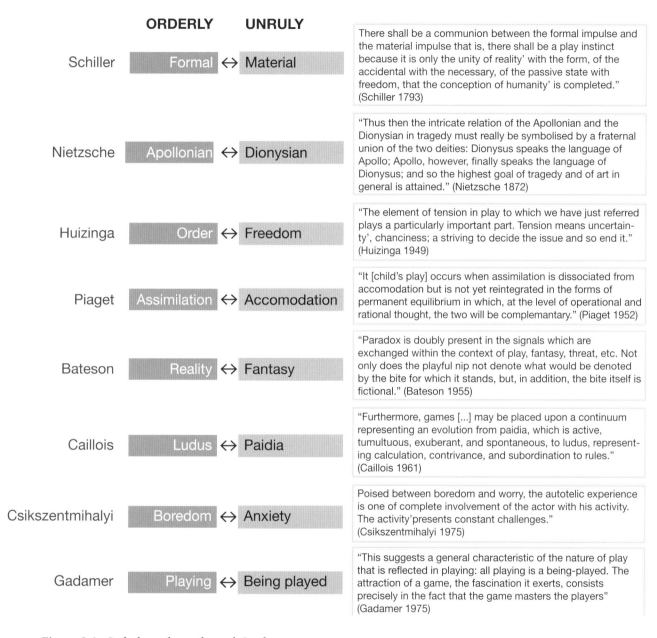

	ORDERLY		**UNRULY**	
Schiller	Formal	↔	Material	"There shall be a communion between the formal impulse and the material impulse that is, there shall be a play instinct because it is only the unity of reality' with the form, of the accidental with the necessary, of the passive state with freedom, that the conception of humanity' is completed." (Schiller 1793)
Nietzsche	Apollonian	↔	Dionysian	"Thus then the intricate relation of the Apollonian and the Dionysian in tragedy must really be symbolised by a fraternal union of the two deities: Dionysus speaks the language of Apollo; Apollo, however, finally speaks the language of Dionysus; and so the highest goal of tragedy and of art in general is attained." (Nietzsche 1872)
Huizinga	Order	↔	Freedom	"The element of tension in play to which we have just referred plays a particularly important part. Tension means uncertainty', chanciness; a striving to decide the issue and so end it." (Huizinga 1949)
Piaget	Assimilation	↔	Accomodation	"It [child's play] occurs when assimilation is dissociated from accomodation but is not yet reintegrated in the forms of permanent equilibrium in which, at the level of operational and rational thought, the two will be complemantary." (Piaget 1952)
Bateson	Reality	↔	Fantasy	"Paradox is doubly present in the signals which are exchanged within the context of play, fantasy, threat, etc. Not only does the playful nip not denote what would be denoted by the bite for which it stands, but, in addition, the bite itself is fictional." (Bateson 1955)
Caillois	Ludus	↔	Paidia	"Furthermore, games [...] may be placed upon a continuum representing an evolution from paidia, which is active, tumultuous, exuberant, and spontaneous, to ludus, representing calculation, contrivance, and subordination to rules." (Caillois 1961)
Csikszentmihalyi	Boredom	↔	Anxiety	"Poised between boredom and worry, the autotelic experience is one of complete involvement of the actor with his activity. The activity'presents constant challenges." (Csikszentmihalyi 1975)
Gadamer	Playing	↔	Being played	"This suggests a general characteristic of the nature of play that is reflected in playing: all playing is a being-played. The attraction of a game, the fascination it exerts, consists precisely in the fact that the game masters the players" (Gadamer 1975)

Figure 3.1: Orderly and unruly explained

nising that all the different theoretical perspectives on the paradoxical duality of play represent a certain tension between *the orderly and the unruly* as shown by Figure 3.1.

While being based on a well-established cross-disciplinary academic body of knowledge, this approach makes for a single general perspective on play that aims to be accessible and useful to play designers by reducing the theoretical complexity to a model that fits the practice of play design as shown in Figure 3.2.

Understanding the Playful Tension Perspective

Based on the above, the Playful Tension perspective proposes that play is characterised by its unique capability to allow for the state of the orderly and the state of the unruly to co-exist by bringing these opposites together and creating tension.

In an orderly state, we feel safe and capable but it may be trivial and mundane, while in the state of the unruly, we feel in danger and incapable and it may be scary for us. In general, we try to live

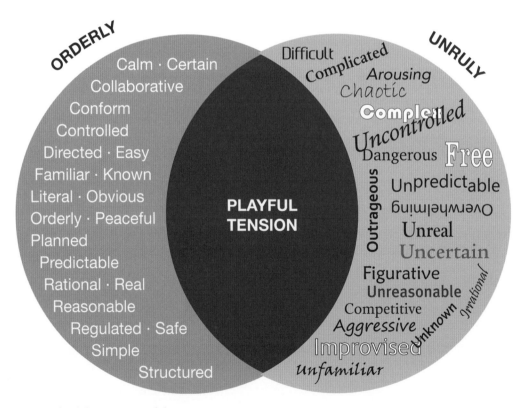

Figure 3.2: Playful tension model

our lives in the state of the orderly knowing what will happen next and what we should do. We create appointments in our calendar, we follow the rules of traffic and we interact with one another according to social conventions. From an evolutionary perspective, we arguably seek the orderly because it increases our chances for survival. We find ourselves in the state of the unruly when things go wrong, when accidents happen or when we are in a situation that we are not equipped to handle. At best, this feels uncomfortable and, at worst, we are run over by a truck.

As much as we want to stay in a state of the orderly, the state of the unruly will present itself sooner or later, so we have to prepare ourselves somehow. This takes us back to the state of play. In play, we are able to create an experience where we allow ourselves to be surprised and to throw ourselves at new challenges while keeping the experience harmless, as play enables the orderly and the unruly states to co-exist.

Play is both orderly and unruly by nature. Too much of one or the other, and the play experience will come to an end. If an experience is too orderly, we know what will happen next, we know exactly what to do, there is no chance of failure, options are limited. If an experience is too unruly, we don't understand what is going on, we become insecure and genuinely scared, behaviour seems irrational, the situation is incomprehensible, options are overwhelming. As a play designer, your job is to help people sustain this double-sided nature of play trying to make sure that the scales don't tip too much in favour of one or the other. The aim is to achieve and sustain a critical point of entropy, or what we may call playful tension.

"Play is characterised by its unique capability to allow for the state of the orderly and the state of the unruly to co-exist by bringing these opposites together and creating tension"

In this perspective, you may think of a play experience as trying to hold two magnets that are repelling one another close together. It creates the powerful force or tension (that equals the central play area in Figure 3.2), but we must exert effort to maintain this tension, or the magnets will slip away from each other. This promotes a view of play as being a volatile state that requires considerable effort to sustain by the players. As play is inherently in danger of breaking down at any moment, it takes both skill and effort to sustain it. Play designers help people initiate and sustain play by designing toys, environments or rule systems that afford playful tension by being simultaneously orderly and unruly.

This playful tension will look different depending on the type of play experience in question. In the following, we will apply the Playful Tension perspective to a few different types of play experiences.

Play Stories

The following are a series of imagined and to some extent idealised and simplified cases of play that serve to illustrate how the Playful Tension perspective can help us to understand the basic dynamics of play and what role play design plays in supporting a play experience. The examples do not by any means cover play in all its nuances but are intended to show how the Playful Tension perspective is applicable to different kinds of play experiences and how you can adopt the perspective as part of your general understanding of play experiences that you create or study.

Physical Play

'Imagine a summer day where a rotating sprinkler is watering a lawn. A group of four girls see the sprinkler and want to play with it. The goal of their game is to not get hit by the shooting water. In prin-

ciple, this would be very easy for the girls to accomplish, as the sprinkler is really not rotating very fast so the kids could easily just place themselves behind it and follow the slow rotation never getting hit by the water. But in this case, the experience would be too orderly to be a good play experience, so the girls don't do this. Instead, they run at the sprinkler from different angles at a high speed, dodging under or jumping over the beam of water in the last minute, laughing and screaming as they succeed or fail. By doing so they create a more unruly experience where they limit their own ability to control and predict how things will play out. They didn't have to do this to achieve the goal of not getting hit by the water, but they had to do it to achieve the playful tension to have themselves a good play experience'.

As the sprinkler story illustrates, people that are inclined to play can create tension between the orderly and the unruly without play designers. But what good play designers do is to make it easier for people to create and maintain this tension. Now if the sprinkler in this story had not been designed with the primary purpose of watering a lawn but rather to be a toy, how could you as a play designer have assisted the kids in maintaining the playful tension? Would you make the sprinkler suddenly change direction? Or speed? Or the angle of the water beam? Or maybe something else entirely?

Gameplay

Moving from physical play to games, we may consider the game of chess. The dynamic looks quite different but relies on the playful tension nonetheless:

'Two men are sitting in a park playing a game of chess. Around them, birds are singing and bees are buzzing, but they don't pay attention to their surroundings. They are sitting in silence staring at the chessboard between them. After a little while, one of the men breaks the silence saying "knight to g5". He moves a horse-shaped piece on the board and hits a button on a clock standing beside the chessboard. The other man responds by scratching his cheek, lowering his eyebrows saying "hmm"'.

In this play story, the physical dimension is not providing anything meaningful to the play experience. Unlike the story of the sprinkler, the chess players are totally orderly. Their bodies and senses are not being put to the test by moving through space feeling the vertigo of the pull of gravity or the wind in their hair; on the contrary, the physical act of picking up and moving the chess pieces is rather uneventful. The play experience of chess relics rather on the playful tension in a cognitive sense. In chess, if you were too capable of determining what would be the optimal move to make, it would make the choice obvious and trivial and the experience would become too orderly by being too predictable, not offering any surprises or uncertainty. On the other hand, the experience would be too unruly if it would be incomprehensible how some moves would be more valuable than others in order to further your chance of victory.

Chess succeeds as a cognitive play experience by creating a playful tension that enables the player to assess the given state of the game and make meaningful predictions about a move while remaining excited to see how things will play out. This is achieved by the playful tension between the orderly and the unruly aspects of the game. Central aspects of chess, such as turn-taking, a clear victory condition, a relatively limited 2-D 8×8 board and consistent rules of movement for each type of chess piece create an order that helps us predict the game and plan our moves. On the other hand, aspects such as the different types of chess pieces all having unique rules of movement, the multiplication of meaningful moves as the pieces come to occupy the entire board, the number of exceptions to the basic movement rules of the individual pieces and (most importantly) the uncertainty of what move the other player will make make up central unruly aspects of the game.

Try asking yourself how you might change the game of chess to maintain the playful tension between players with different levels of skill.

Fantasy Play

If we leave the rule-bound gameplay of chess in favour of narrative fantasy play, we get yet another dimension of playful tension.

'A boy is playing with a toy robot. "Pew pew". The boy pretends that the robot shoots deadly lasers from its eyes. The robot attacks a toy farm and begins to kill the different toy animals while the boy makes vigorous sound effects. "Arrrrrgh. Noooo not the sheep!" The farmer tries to ram the robot with a blue tractor, to no effect. "Call the army!" the boy says in the voice of the farmer. "Ok", says the boy in a higher voice while grabbing and shaking his sister's Barbie doll, who is playing the part of the farmer's wife even though the doll is very big compared to the other toys in play. Finally, a toy tank rolls in and destroys the robot in dramatic fashion.'

Here, the toys serve to achieve playful tension by making the play experience more orderly. The design of the toys carries a meaning that the boy can use to guide his decisions as he improvises the narrative. If the boy had only stones at his disposal, they would not have provided the same kind of stabilising direction and inspiration for improvising the play narrative. It would still be possible for the boy to sustain narrative play only with stones, but if the relationship between the play object and the narrative is so abstract that the stones potentially could represent any-thing, the possibilities would easily become too many to navigate and the play experience would become quite unruly. In that case, all the creative responsibility falls on the boy to sustain the play experience and keep the narrative from collapsing into meaninglessness. A well-designed toy promotes order and helps maintain playful tension in narrative play by enforcing certain narratives and neglecting others to sustain play by limiting the possibility space of what can meaningfully happen next, while providing enough options to make it exciting to see how the story plays out.

In fantasy play, the improvised stories tend to revolve around characters that resolve conflict and try to achieve goals. What are some of your own memories of your favourite toys for fantasy play, and how were these designed to inspire you to come up with interesting conflicts and goals for your stories?

Construction Play

Finally, let's extend the creative play from the narrative fantasy play to an instance of physical construction play.

'A boy approaches a big pile of LEGO bricks wanting to build something cool but not knowing exactly what to build yet. He runs his hands through the bricks looking at all the different shapes and colours. "What should I make?" Suddenly, a brick grabs his attention. It is a big wheel with a

rubber tyre on a white rim. "Maybe I could make a space buggy!" The boy searches through the pile of bricks for more wheels of the same type but is only able to find three in total. "Maybe it should be a space motorbike with three wheels instead". The boy begins constructing the bike using more generic bricks to create the chassis to hold the wheels. While searching for a piece he comes across a rowboat piece that he finds interesting. The rowboat has a pirate cannon mounted on it already from previous play. "Maybe it could somehow fit on the space bike?" The boy makes some adjustments to the chassis and mounts the boat and cannon. "It is a space-pirate bike!" The boy goes on to look for pieces to build a space-pirate mini-figure. "He needs a wooden peg and a black space helmet"'.

In this scenario, the huge amount of different LEGO bricks introduces the unruly to the experience by offering countless possibilities and making it uncertain if you will find the pieces that you are looking for. The affordances of the individual bricks create the orderly when they inspire the direction of the build. Generic bricks like the classic 2×4 LEGO bricks are open and do not impose much direction on their own. In the example, the big wheels, the rowboat and the cannon, on the other hand, are all pieces that carry specific meaning and, as such, they become catalyst pieces that have a big impact on the build and create order in doing so.

The storytelling also adds order by constantly re-evaluating what is being built and what bricks are relevant to look for and add to the build. The LEGO bricks create a playful tension by structuring the build and offering direction while simultaneously making seemingly anything possible and letting you surprise yourself by suddenly changing the direction of the build.

If you get the chance to build something with LEGO bricks, try reflecting on your own creative process considering the dynamic between your creative decisions and the design of the specific bricks that you are playing with.

Using the Playful Tension Perspective

By now you should have a good idea of what we mean when we talk about play experiences as a playful tension between the orderly and the unruly. This brings us to the big question; how can you use this perspective in your play design practice?

In the context of the LEGO House play design team, this is done by printing posters with the model (Figure 3.2) to let the team collaborate in mapping how a given play design affords playful tension by identifying key elements that afford order or unruliness. Each element is put on a sticky note and placed on the poster to create a mapping of the playful tension as shown by Figure 3.3.

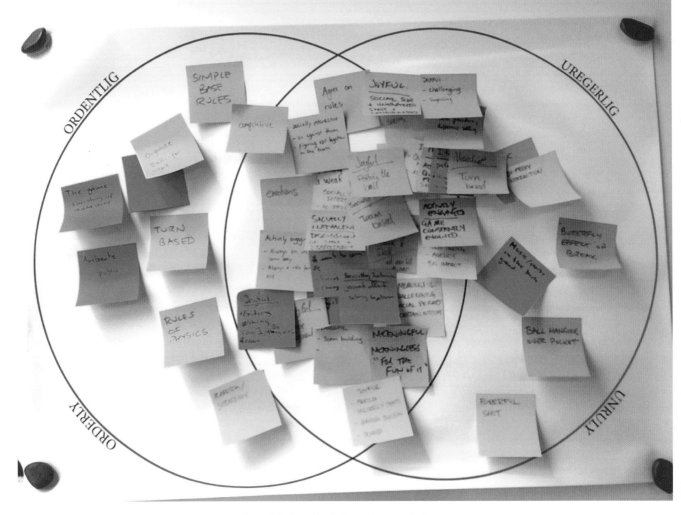

Figure 3.3: Poster creative exercise with the playful tension model

This process is useful for examining and understanding existing play experiences, concept development, and concept evaluation.

Beginning with the first, the perspective of playful tension can be used as a framework for the analysis of existing play experiences as demonstrated, albeit superficially, by the previous play stories. This is useful whenever you need to understand what makes trending play experiences successful. Maybe you are a game developer that needs to understand what makes *Fortnite* so popular or a toy designer that wants to understand kids' fascination with *Squishies*, or maybe you are just curious to learn what makes *Hide and Seek* a classic play experience. The playful tension perspective lets you analyse any kind of existing play experience and learn what makes them work by examining how each element of the design works to create playful tension. This can be valuable knowledge to bring into the beginning phases of your own design process as part of understanding your target group's favourite play experiences and for defining design principles for your project.

During concept development, where initial ideas are being explored, expanded and defined, mapping of playful tension on the poster is useful in order to articulate and improve the play experience that you are designing for. Just as with the analysis of existing play experiences you identify the elements of your design that would shape the play experience and map how each element works to create playful tension. Try asking yourself or discuss with your team: how is our design creating playful tension? The playful tension often works across several dimensions of the play experience even if some are more important than others. Thinking back to the play stories above, they show how playful tension differs across physical, cognitive and creative play. Considering how your design affords playful tension across various dimensions of the play experience will help you to be aware of how your design is intended to inspire and support play. This will enable you to know why your play design is working or not once you begin user testing. You could also apply the playful tension perspective in your idea development phase to create design alternatives by asking: what are the different ways in which you

could make a given idea more unruly? And subsequently, how would you create order to maintain playful tension given the increased unruliness?

> " Considering how your design affords playful tension across various dimensions of the play experience will help you to be aware of how your design is intended to inspire and support play "

Once you have a working prototype of your play design and begin testing it with users, the playful tension perspective will help you evaluate your test results. You do this by looking for the moments where the play experience breaks down due to boredom, confusion, stress, fatigue, etc. For each of these breakdowns, you analyse why the playful tension failed – did the play experience get too orderly or too unruly and in what sense? The individual breakdown may be due to the specific player's unique personal preferences and tolerances in terms of playful tension, but if you notice the same type of breakdown across multiple tests with different users, you should consider how to change your play design in order to better afford and maintain playful tension.

Quick Take-Aways

Thinking about the practice of play design as an effort to help players create and maintain playful tension allows play designers to develop their ideas in consideration of the paradoxical double-sided nature of play. Play designers can work with the Playful Tension perspective by putting the playful tension model on a poster or on a whiteboard and reflect on how various design elements affords playful tension by adding either order or unruliness to the play experience by mapping the elements onto the model using sticky notes.

Further Reading

Bateson, G. (1955). A Theory of Play and Fantasy. In *Steps to an Ecology of Mind: Collected Essays in Anthropology, Psychiatry, Evolution, and Epistemology*. Chicago, Illinois: University of Chicago Press.

Caillois, R. (1961). *Man, Play, and Games.* University of Illinois Press.

Csikszentmihalyi, M. (1975). *Beyond Boredom and Anxiety: Experiencing Flow in Work and Play*. San Francisco. Jossey-Bass.

Gadamer, H. (1975). *Truth and Method.* Sheed & Ward Ltd and the Continuum Publishing Group.

Huizinga, J. (1949). *Homo Ludens: A Study of the Play-element in Culture.* Routledge & Kegan Paul. London, Boston and Henley.

Nietzsche, F. (1872). *The Birth of Tragedy.* In *The Complete Works of Friedrich Nietzsche, Volume 1,* Edited by Dr Oscar Levy. London: The Macmillan company.

Piaget, J. (1952). *Play, Dreams and Imitation in Childhood.* New York, NY, US: W W Norton & Co.

Schiller, F. (1793). Letters Upon The Aesthetic Education of Man. In Schiller Institute *Friedrich Schiller, poet of freedom.* Schiller Institute. New Benjamin Franklin House. New York.

Acknowledgement

I would like to thank LEGO House and the LEGO Foundation for their collaboration in developing the Playful Tension perspective.

Play Design Insight 4:

Designing Play Solutions with the Lenses of Play Card Tool

Tilde Bekker, Ben Schouten & Linda de Valk

This chapter will present a design tool, called the Lenses of Play, that provides five different perspectives when designing (digital) play solutions. The five play perspectives include designing for 1) forms of play, 2) open-ended play, 3) playful experiences, 4) stages of play and 5) emergence of play over time. The Lenses of Play is a card-based design tool, consisting of a total of twenty-six cards that provide design knowledge. When designing for play, a designer can switch between and combine these different perspectives to develop a rich play solution. The tool is useful for teaching design students how and when to consider different design perspectives in a design process. It can also be used by (experienced) play designers to ideate, evaluate and present play design considerations to make the different perspectives and qualities of play explicit.

Introduction

The concept and process of play have been examined in various disciplines, such as child development, philosophy, anthropology, cultural studies, media studies and sociology. When designing for play, you can be inspired by theories and concepts from these different disciplines. Different theories can allow you, as a designer, to explore different scenarios of use, and different framings of play. By exploring the inspiration of the different framings, this can provide an opportunity to design in-depth solutions, grounded in theoretical knowledge, that provide a more extensive play experience, than a play experience that is interesting for a limited amount of time. We will examine a number of different perspectives that one might take when examining play using a scenario-based design approach.

> " Emergence and strategy are examples of how play scenarios can evolve over time, balancing, opening up and narrowing down the play space and its possible procedures, stories and scenarios. "

Imagine this Play Scenario

'Mark, Susie and John are playing in a sandbox in the garden. Mark is playing with a truck and is making engine sounds to get the attention of Susie, who is also playing in the sandbox. John and Susie have created a mountain out of the sand, with tracks for marbles to roll down. After playing in the sandpit for ten minutes, Mark feels like changing to a different kind of game. He wants to combine the use of the truck and the marbles somehow. Mark suggests this to Susie and John, and after some chatting, Susie starts to adjust the track on the mountain of sand, so that the truck can also ride down the mountain.'

If we examine this scenario, we can see that there are many aspects to play and that it is a very dynamic process. John and Susie are engaged in free play activities (unstructured activity). They have come up with their own play activities and have developed some rules (open-ended play), inspired by some of the objects and environmental properties. They like building things (creative play form) and moving around in the sandbox (physical play form). They also like to create challenges for themselves (challenge: playful experience) and playing together (collaboration; playful experience). They like playing together and they negotiate different play goals and what rules are acceptable (social play). The way in which they play develops over time: they switch between exploring the opportunities of the environment (exploration play stage), developing more complex play activities (immersion play stage). This can be temporarily interrupted by inviting in a new player (invitation play stage).

Different Perspectives on Play

Where can we look for theories that provide inspiration when designing for play? As an overall model for designing for playful interactions, we can examine the MDA (Mechanics, Dynamics, Aesthetics) model by Hunicke et al. (2014). The mechanics are the components of the (play) system, the dynamics are the behaviours that flow from interacting with the (rules) in the system, and the aesthetics describe the emotional response or player experience. The model describes the relationship between games as systems and games as player experience [3, p. 2]: *'From the designer's perspective, the mechanics give rise to dynamic system behaviour, which in turn leads to particular aesthetic experiences. From the player's perspective, aesthetics set the tone, which is born out in observable dynamics and eventually, operable mechanics'.* The MDA model can also be used to examine designing play solutions (Bekker et al. 2014). Components of a play environment include the players, the objects and the environment.

Play is a process that develops over time, guided by its mechanics. For instance, when we play football, the simple necessity of kicking the ball in the net to score, brings forth diverse dynamics, such as strategies and tactics, rules that emerge, like 'offsides' or other. Emergence and strategy are examples of how play scenarios can evolve over time, balancing, opening up and narrowing down the play space and its possible procedures, stories and scenarios. When looking at it from an experience point of view, as play develops, several emotions might also evolve over time.

Play and Digital Media

Play is an activity that can be mediated in digital entertainment games, but also has other opportunities to come alive, such as through toys, tabletop games, storytelling, etc. In co-existence with the strong development of entertainment games since the late '60s of the last century, digital play becomes an essential of daily life. Digital objects can be designed to create opportunities for various user groups, such as children, to engage in specific activities, allowing children to practice skills and, or just to enjoy themselves. Digital objects, by its embedded sensors, actuators and data acquisition can detect user behaviour, provide feedback and provide feed forward (Mironcika et al. 2018) and scaffold the play dynamics according to personal skills and contexts (unbalanced versus balanced play). They can adjust their behaviour to user behaviour. They can provide opportunities for meaning-making through stories or scenarios, creativity, fantasy play, but also for social interaction, negotiating and sharing practices.

We will illustrate the potential of digital play environment explaining an interaction scenario with the GlowSteps (see Figure 4.1). GlowSteps (Valk et al. 2013b) is an open-ended, interactive play environment that consists of interactive tiles that react with light output on the player's actions.

'Lisa and Dave are playing with Glow-Steps. Lisa points at the green light: "We have to step on green!" She jumps over the tiles towards the green light. Dave runs over the floor and is faster at the light than Lisa. "You're out", she says. "You are not allowed to touch the floor". Dave shrugs his shoulders but does not protest. After a while, their friend Mike joins them.

He likes to obstruct Dave and Lisa. Dave makes a diversion and tricks Mike. He cheers and Lisa shouts: "Yes!" when Dave jumps on the green light'.

In this scenario, Lisa comes up with the goal of stepping on the green light. She also mentions the rule that stepping on the ground is not allowed. The scenario shows competitive play (Lisa and Dave trying to be the first to step on the green light and Mike obstructing them) and cooperative play (Lisa cheering for Dave when he catches the green light).

The Lenses of Play as a Design Tool

The Lenses of Play approach is a design framework that provides a set of lenses that play designers and facilitators can use in thinking about play solutions. The Lenses of Play is a card-based design tool, consisting of a total of twenty-six cards that provide design knowledge.

Play can be seen from various perspectives. These can all be inspirational and informative. In design, it is good to switch from one perspective to the next to examine how to develop a well-balanced interactive solution that is suitable for the context and user groups and is appealing for a longer period.

The five play lenses include:

1. **Open-ended play**. This perspective is related to properties of play such as the amount of structure that is provided, whether (end) goals have been defined, to what extent the rules are fixed, and the flexibility to allocate meaning to the play activity (see Figure 4.2). It describes the space between more rule-based activities (also called Ludus) and free play (also called paidia). This lens is grounded in game theory about rules that can be more defined in the mechanics (such as in chess) or emerging from its (physical) properties, such as in the case of toys (Valk et al. 2013).

Figure 4.1: Glowsteps

2. **Forms of play.** This lens is informed by different types or forms of behaviour that children and adults can engage in. Different forms of play include, constructive or creative play, pretend or socio-dramatic play, physical or active play and play with provided and invented rules. This lens is grounded in child development, game and play theories (Bekker et al. 2014a).

3. **Stages of play.** This perspective addresses the fact that play can go through three different phases (see Figure 4.3). How does play start and how does it end? The first stage is related to considerations about how play contexts can invite players to start playing. The second stage of exploration covers how players slowly discover the opportunities for play, such as how to incorporate different objects, players and storylines. The third stage includes how a play environment can provide more complex interactions between players, objects and meaning; where players become fully immersed in the interaction. This lens is grounded in communication and interaction theories and models (Valk et al. 2015).

4. **Playful experiences**. This lens addresses play from the user experience

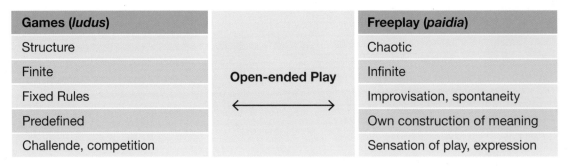

Games (*ludus*)	Open-ended Play	Freeplay (*paidia*)
Structure		Chaotic
Finite		Infinite
Fixed Rules	←→	Improvisation, spontaneity
Predefined		Own construction of meaning
Challende, competition		Sensation of play, expression

Figure 4.2: Open-ended play

perspective. It supports the designer in designing for specific experiences, such as discovery, challenge, relatedness or sympathy. This lens is very closely related to the playful experience list developed by Korhonen et al. (2009). The lens includes philosophical, psychological and game design perspectives (Bekker et al. 2014b).

5. **Emergence of play.** This lens addresses the dynamic nature of play. They include emergence principles, which are examples of emergent behaviour observed in nature or culture, such as swarming and clustering. They also include emergence parameters, which include characteristics that influence the dynamic behaviour, such as visibility, predictability and relatedness. This lens is grounded in theories about behaviour in nature and cultural systems (Rijnbout et al. 2013).

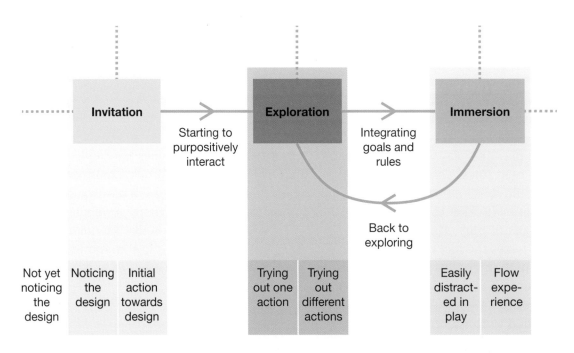

Figure 4.3: Stages of interaction

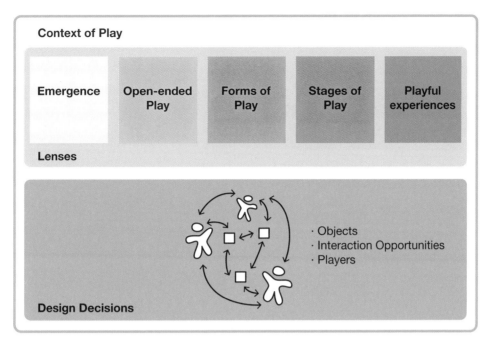

Figure 4.4: The use of the lenses of play related to design decisions

Development of the Lenses of Play Tool

The Lenses of Play framework was developed iteratively over the course of a period of 6 years. During this process design, researchers and design students developed a wide range of digital play solutions for different user groups and play contexts, sometimes in collaborations with companies, including Kompan, KLM, Janssen Fritsen and NYON. Some examples of designs that were made are: an outdoor digital play object to motivate teenagers to be physically active, an indoor play environment to support young children's phantasy play (called Wobble), an interactive version of the 'ball-pit' for shops such as IKEA, a wayfinding system for families in a hospital and a decentralised play environment to support social and physical play (GlowSteps). Over time we examined how different theories and knowledge can inspire design decision making. Through design analyses of designs made, the design knowledge was gathered and represented in a card-based design tool, called the Lenses of Play.

Using the Lenses of Play Tool During Different Phases of a Design Project

An important quality of play is its open-ended nature. That open-endedness has often been a starting point in our own design research projects. Some of the challenges of designing for play include: to design for an activity that has an open structure, can be flexible in how it develops over time, provides diverse and shifting experiences, incorporates multiple forms of play, and provides subtle triggers that are meaningful and appropriate given the history and the development of the play activity. An important challenge of designing for open-ended play is how to find a balance between, on the one hand, providing some triggers for play and some minimal structure and, on the other hand, not to provide too much structure but leave enough room for improvisation.

Designing for play can be done for diverse design intentions, such as supporting social interaction, playful learning or motivating physical activity. These intentions must match the qualities and opportunities that playful interaction can offer.

Designing for play requires a very iterative design process, in which design ideas are tried out, as it is difficult to determine how the opportunities created will be used by users in specific contexts. The Lenses of Play can be used as a framework for framing, ideation, concept development and evaluation of play solutions. By examining the different perspectives/ lenses designers can explore how to develop a rich and flexible play solution.

Questions to ask about using the Lenses of Play are:
· When do you use, which lens?
· How many lenses to use?
· Do you use the lenses for designing play solutions, for teaching how to design play solutions or for analysing play behaviours?

> " An important challenge of designing for open-ended play is how to find a balance between, on the one hand, providing some triggers for play and some minimal structure and, on the other hand, not to provide too much structure but leave enough room for improvisation. "

Overall, open-ended play is a design quality that needs to be decided on *early in the design process* as it guides some basic design decisions about how play opportunities are provided by the play objects. However, in different phases of the design process, reflecting on whether the design still meets this play quality is important. Forms of play is another lens that can be helpful early in the design process for exploring design directions and framing a design brief. The set of playful experiences can also be a starting point to think about how something might be playful. Is it because there is a surprise, unexpectedness or exploration or because there is competition or collaboration?

In *a middle design phase*, the design needs to be developed further including more extensive and diverse play scenarios, with diverse interaction possibilities. In the middle, you can still have multiple designs and you want to select the most promising one. Or you have a very broad concept that you want to narrow down. At that point, the stages of interaction start playing a role. It supports examining diverse stages of interaction, and also possible shifts between different play experiences.

Then in a *later design stage*, the design can be further developed, by looking again at opportunities for further detailing, (or simplifying) the interaction opportunities. In the later phases, you make more detailed decisions e.g. fine-tuning interaction behaviour.

The Lenses of Play can be used in different ways, including for designing for play and for teaching how to design for play. These two cases are explained in the following two sections.

Case 1: Wobble

How the Lenses of Play are used throughout the design process.

This design case intends to show how the Lenses of Play were used to develop a digital play environment intended to stimulate fantasy play of young children (for more details about the design case, see Valk et al. 2015). The design of Wobble was made by Alice van de Beukering (then an Industrial Design master student). She developed Wobble by going through three user-centred design phases.

In the *early design phase*, the designer decided to focus on pretend and fantasy play (forms of play), and on the playful experiences of magic, surprise and fellowship (playful experiences). She decided to provide open-ended play opportunities through balls with light feedback and sounds (open-ended play).

In *the middle design phase* design explorations were made around different interaction scenarios. The overall focus on the forms of play stayed the same: fantasy play. To support improvisation in open-ended play, some concrete objects, e.g. ladybugs and butterflies, were added to Wobble (see Figure 4.5). The evaluations in the early phase showed Wobble was too abstract for children to start coming up with some game ideas. The interaction rules were also varied to explore how to enhance the playful experiences of exploration and curiosity.

In *the later design phase,* a decision was made to provide more handles for fantasy play in open-ended play context: e.g. provide graphical help on the balls because young children need more concrete pointers for fantasy play and more clear rules for stages of play. Furthermore, a new interaction rule was added about the balls changing colour if not touched for a while providing new opportunities for open-ended play.

83

Figure 4.5: Children playing with the fantasy play environment wobble

Case 2

Teaching how to design for digital play to bachelor engineering students.

We use the Lenses of Play in a bachelor course for students at a technical university, including computer science, mechanical engineering and industrial design students. The students are taught how theories, through e.g. the Lenses of Play card tool, can inform developing tangible play solutions, such as interactive student backpacks that support students to engage in playful social interaction.

Learning objectives of the bachelor course include:

· Being able to analyse playful applications using various play theories and frameworks
· Being able to explain and apply play design perspectives, such as those described in the Lenses of Play tool
· Being able to design, build and programme an interesting digital tangible play solution in a distributed intelligent environment
· Being able to plan, carry out and interpret the outcome of user tests of tangible play solutions

They apply the lenses related to a design brief that asks them to develop interactive digital tangible playful solutions.

They are first introduced to the continuum of *closed* and *open-ended play* and *playful experiences*. To get a basic understanding of how to use some play frameworks, they analyse an existing digital playful solution, such as the interactive piano stairs developed by Volkswagen using the Fun Theory (see: https://www.designoftheworld.com/piano-stairs/). This gives them a sense of how other designers have incorporated playful qualities, and why the design decisions are suitable for a specific context.

They then start exploring how to design a tangible play solution for a specific context. They start by selecting a few *playful experiences* that seem appropriate for the context and explore various *open-ended solutions.*

Students informally evaluate with users, how they perceive the playful experience and the interaction with the design.

They then explore whether they can enrich the design by analysing whether different *forms of play* would provide a richer interaction scenario. Then they further develop their design by examining how to provide a longer-lasting, more diverse and more dynamic interaction, by using the stages of play lens. Finally, they must do another informal user test to examine whether their expectations about the play behaviour turn out as they intended, and how the users experience the play solution.

Overall, our experience is that the lenses that represent different perspectives give the students a wide set of theoretical knowledge to inspire their design. Furthermore, having the students switch between the perspectives allows them to develop quite rich interaction scenarios in a fairly short time.

Reflective Questions When Using the Lenses of Play Tool

Designing with the Lenses of Play:

- What *playful experiences* are appropriate for the context that you are de-

signing or using them for? How have you determined and verified this?
- How does your design support different *play opportunities over time?*
- Where have you set the balance between openness in the play activity and providing some triggers and structure in the play activity?

"having the students switch between the perspectives allows them to develop quite rich interaction scenarios in a fairly short time."

- Explore how applying different *forms of play*, or different combinations of forms of play guide the design solution in different directions in an idea generation session.
- Conduct a design analysis of some existing designs, or play observation data, to examine what different *play experiences* you interpret are perceived by the players and how they shift over time? In relation to this, you can examine what are possible contributors to the experiences arising in the play activity?
- After having created an initial play design, examine how the interactive behaviour can vary to support the

different *stages of interaction*: how are players invited to join in the interaction, how does the design support exploring what is possible, and how can different play patterns emerge and flow for a slightly longer period?

· Explore how *open-endedness* can be supported in relation to different design decisions: for example, is the feed forward and feedback interpretable in different ways, can there be a negotiation between players about how interaction behaviour of the system is interpreted, and are there multiple paths and end goals possible?

Teaching with the Lenses of Play:

· How will you ask the students to apply the Lenses of Play in the different phases of the design process?
· Will the students be allowed to decide by themselves how many and which lenses and cards to apply, or are you going to pre-structure these decisions?
· The considerations mentioned above, about designing with the Lenses of Play, can be used to phrase educational exercises.

Quick Take-Aways

This play design insight chapter has presented the Lenses of Play tool and has illustrated how the lenses provide different perspectives when designing for play. How the different lenses can best be used also depends on the context of use, such as to which design project it is being applied, or how it is used for teaching purposes. The lenses can be used separately, or in combination, for a variety of design activities, such as analysing existing designs, brainstorming new concepts, extending existing play designs and explaining core design decisions to others. The Lenses of Play can certainly be extended by other design knowledge that presents even different perspectives on play and can be combined with other design methods for developing play concepts.

Further Reading

A copy of The Lenses of Play Card Tool can be requested through the first author of the chapter.

Bekker, T, Schouten, B & Graaf, M. de. (2014). Designing Interactive Tangible Games for Diverse Forms of Play. *In Handbook of Digital Games*. Eds. Marios C. Angelides and Harry Agius, John Wiley & Sons, Inc., 710-729.

Bekker, T, Valk, L. de & Eggen, B. (2014). A Toolkit for Designing Playful Interactions: the Four Lenses of Play. *Journal of Ambient Intelligence and Smart Environments (JAISE),* 6 (3), 263-276.

Bergen, D. (1998). Play as a Medium for Learning and Development. *Association for Childhood Education International.*

Hunicke, R., M. LeBlanc & R. Zubek. (2004). MDA: A formal Approach to Game Design and Game Research. *Proc. AAAI Workshop on Challenges in Game*. AAAI Press, San Jose, CA, 2004.

Korhonen, H, M. Montola & J. Arrasvuori, (2009). Understanding Playful Experiences Through Digital Games. *Proc. on Designing Pleasurable Products and Interface*, Compiègne, France. pp. 274–285.

Mironcika, S., de Schipper, A., Brons, A., Toussaint, H., Kröse, B., & Schouten, B. (2018). Smart Toys Design Opportunities for measuring Children's fine Motor Skills Development. In *Proceedings of the Twelfth International Conference on Tangible, Embedded, and Embodied Interaction*. PP. 349-356.

Resnick, M. (2007). All I really Need to Know (About Creative Thinking) I Iearned (by Studying how Children Learn) in Kindergarten. *In Proceedings of the 6th ACM SIGCHI Conference on Creativity & cognition* (C&C '07). ACM, New York, NY, USA, 1-6.

Rijnbout, P., de Valk, L., Vermeeren, A., Bekker, T., de Graaf, M., Schouten, B., & Eggen, B. (2013). About Experience and Emergence-A Framework for Decentralised Interactive Play Environments. *In Intelligent Technologies for Interactive Entertainment* (pp. 104-113). Springer International Publishing.

Salen, K. & Zimmerman, E. (2003). *Rules of Play: Game Design Fundamentals.* Cambridge, MA: The MIT Press.

Valk, L. de, Bekker, T. & Eggen, B. (2015). Designing for Social Interaction in Open-ended Play Environments. *International Journal of Design,* 9 (1), 107-120.

Valk, L. de, Bekker, T. & Eggen, B. (2013). Leaving Room for Improvisation: Towards a Design Approach for Open-ended Play. *In Proceedings of the 12th International Conference on Interaction Design and Children* (IDC '13). ACM, New York, NY, USA, 92-101.

Acknowledgement

We could like to thank our (former) colleagues Berry Eggen, Mark de Graaf and Pepijn Rijnbout for jointly developing the Lenses of Play.

Play Design Insight 5:

Designing for Play with a child-centred Design Approach

Karen Feder

This chapter introduces the child-centred design approach that enables designers to take the perspective of children when designing for play. By taking the starting point in the children instead of the product, makes it possible to ensure a high degree of relevancy in the design – seen from the perspective of the children. The child-centred design approach encourages the designers to participate in the children's everyday lives to gain an understanding of what they are designing for. For doing this, the chapter presents three child-centred design methods; internship as a child, co-creating the life of a child and comparing child-personas, all of them with the purpose of acknowledging the child as the expert – the expert of being a child.

Introduction: Why Taking on a Child-Centred Design Approach

As adults we can tend to think that designing for children is easy since we all have been a child once... but does our childhood makes us experts of being a child nowadays? Do we actually know how children live their lives today? Do we know their interest or what they like to play and with whom? Are we able to take the perspective of a child when designing for children? Or is our design approach based upon our often out-of-date perception of children, our assumptions on children's everyday life or originated from our own opinion on what is best for the children?

More and more designers and companies have discovered the value of focusing on the user. The implementation of user-centred design methods, like personas, focus groups and user-testing, is growing, and so are the development and education in these kinds of methods. Despite the increasing interest in the user, the user is still often looked at from the perspective of the designer (Feder 2013). In participatory design, we invite the user to participate in different ways – but often as being a part of our design process, in our design studios using our design methods for the purpose of designing our product.

What if we switch this perspective around, by inviting ourselves into the everyday lives of children, in their everyday surroundings, commit to their daily activities – to get a sense of the context that we are designing for? To take on the perspective of the child – to see the world through their eyes. As a way to gain more accurate knowledge and a deeper insight into the children that we are designing for and to obtain an understanding of their everyday life seen from their perspective – even though it may collide with our expectation, beliefs and world view. This clash can help us to take a stand when we are designing since it offers us the opportunity to move away from our 'I-believe-I-know-what-the-children-needs-and-wants' and into a more respectful way of designing with a child-centred design approach (Feder 2020).

This way of working requires courage and nerve – and that we dare to set our own profession aside. We will have to be curious, open-minded and impartial to experience the world from the children's perspective. We will need the ability to be human, honest and sincere in our interaction with the children and our engagement in their everyday life. This calls for specific tools, methods, approaches and maybe most of all a mindset that supports this way of working, acting and thinking.

The child-centred design approach presented in this chapter offers tools and methods to work with a child-centred design approach when designing for play. Tools to approach the life of children, methods that explain the value of conducting child-centred design activities in a design process and an approach that let you take a stand when going into a development process. All of them supporting the growth of a child-centred mindset that makes us aware of the opportunity and importance of designing with a child-centred design approach when designing for play for children.

> " It is about being present in the moment, without any other agenda than a sincere interest in the children, how they live their lives, what they take an interest in and what they see as important in their life. It is to acknowledge the child as the expert – the expert on being a child. "

WHAT is a Child-Centred Design Approach

When designing for play experiences for children, a child-centred design approach offers the opportunity to take the starting point in children – as opposed to the product, the designer, the company, the parents or other stakeholders. This can be a way to make sure the final play experience is relevant for the children in the context that they are a part of. 'Relevant' is in this case as seen from the child's perspective, which is not always similar to what an adult sees as relevant for the child. This approach offers the designer the opportunity to see the world through the eyes of a child and by that designing play experiences from the perspective of a child – with the child and for the child.

The child-centred design approach is leading our attention to the child and their everyday life when designing for children. It emphasises the importance of the child as the end-user of the play experience by demanding we take that into consideration in our design process. When designing with a child-centred design approach we take the starting point in children, we let ourselves be inspired by children, we play with children, we learn through children and then we will ask ourselves: 'What would make sense to design – seen from the perspective of the child?'.

To design with a child-centred design approach is all about being in it together with the children – on their turf (Ackermann 2013) and not just relying on books, reports and studies on children. It demands that we leave our offices, our design studios, our safe spots and walk out into the real lives of children. It is all about spending time together with children in the places they like to be and do the things they like to do. It is creating the space, the time and the atmosphere that brings the perspective of the child to the foreground. It is about being present in the moment, without any other agenda than a sincere interest in the children, how they live their lives, what they take an interest in and what they see as important in their life. It is to acknowledge the child as the expert – the expert on being a child.

For us as designers, the child-centred design approach urges us to meet the children halfway. To get together as equals and do things together that we have in common. Designers and children both like to make and to build which offers us the opportunity to create together – create ideas, activities and things together, as well as knowledge, awareness and respect. Together we have the potential to imagine the future, what it should look like and how we would like to live in it.

For us to be aware of the potential of children, we will have to face our own assumptions and confront our usual perception of children. We will have to engage in activities that challenge our view and leaves room for surprises. We need to let go of the control, go with the flow and let the children lead the way, to really reach the full potential of a child-centred design approach. Even though we cannot know what to come out of it from the start. We will have to trust the process, the methods and our own ability to see the potential in the unexplored space we are moving into together with the children. Not just to gain exact insights on the specific children we are working with, but to gain an understanding of children in general for knowing who we are designing for. And not just to inform one specific development process, but to achieve a general understanding also valuable for the coming design processes.

The following sections introduce three child-centred design methods exemplified through relevant cases.

Internship as a Child

As a part of a professional development course a number of professional design practitioners from different companies and organisations were introduced to the child-centred design method; 'Internship as a child'. The purpose of the internship was to offer the designers the opportunity to learn through experience (Kolb 1984) in the everyday life of children (Pellegrini 2013) by engaging in their daily activities (Gunn, Otto, & Smith 2013). An encouragement to spend time together with the children on the children's terms – to become aware of who they are designing for and the context they are designing to.

The designers were invited in as interns in the children's familiar surroundings outside school; their private homes and their after-school club, where the children felt safe and free to act how they normally would do and prefer to. The more in control the child is in the setting, the higher is the potential for gaining a child-perspective. It can be more difficult to experience the children's perspective in a school setting with a fixed educational structure and controlling teachers, than for example at a playground or at the children's private houses. The designers were introduced to the children as play designers who design for children as their professional job and the reason for them to be there is because they wanted to know more about how it is to be a child. The children were told that they were the experts – the experts on being children – and that they should just be themselves and act like they normally would on any given day, even though the designers would tag along and be in it together with them in their everyday activities.

'The children were really keen on showing me stuff and telling me about their lives – they were on their home turf and liked to be the host'. – Participating designer

The children easily took on the role of hosts for the interns, and the designers were included in the activities on equal terms. That meant that the designers had to shed some of their 'professionalism' to grasp by intuition what they were experiencing with the children. They had to fol-

low the children's lead and do the same things as them; jumping the trampoline, fixing a skateboard or putting on nail polish. The designers were not just observers – they had to be active participants in the children's life. Therefore, they couldn't act as a designer usually would do in a situation like this; writing down notes and taking photos, while being an intern. They had to do the same as the children – and children are not taking notes while living their lives.

'The girl showed me her room and told me a lot about all the social media she was a part of – I was very surprised by how familiar she was in this area… she is only 9 years old!' – Participating designer

Even though the designers didn't take any notes or photos, they were taught how to make mental notes for later by embracing their experiences in the moment. Right after the internship as a child, they were encouraged to reflect upon their experiences. They wrote down their reflections, their experiences, their thoughts and their ideas. They also wrote down if something surprised them since that is often a sign of challenged preconceptions, new insights or a hidden potential for something interesting and innovative. The reflection process (Schon 1983) is an important part of becoming aware of the value of the child-centred design approach; how children can inspire us to design from their point of view, how it can stimulate and motivate us to step aside from a product-centred or designer-centred approach, how it can encourage us to acknowledge children's role in the development process, how it influences us as designers as well as our perception of children, and how it impacts the relevance of the final design.

'It is important to visit kids like this because it is obvious that their childhood is very different from ours'. – Participating designer

The designers became aware of how much they actually did not know about children, and how important it was to go out in the children's everyday lives to experience them in their familiar surroundings. It opened up their eyes for how open and honest the children are and how they are the real experts on how it is to be a child.

Co-Creating the Life of a Child

A group of educated designers participated in a research project on developing a child-centred design approach, specifically a co-creation method, which could offer the designer a more in-depth understanding of children's lives – as seen from the children's perspective. The intention was to develop a more child-friendly method for establishing a dialogue between designers and children, through the use of generative toolkits (Brandt et al. 2013; Sanders & Stappers 2014). The partici-

pation (Hart 1992) aimed at taking the children's ability, competences and preferences more into account than a regular interview normally does.

The participating children were divided into small groups with one designer in each of the groups, with the purpose of making a more equal power balance between children and adult. The groups were introduced to the co-creation activity and were asked to build the life of a child with the provided materials. The children accepted the challenge right away, whereas the adult designers in the groups were more hesitant and raised clarifying questions before accepting the task.

'For one like me, it is very challenging to go into a process like this, if I don't know why or what is supposed to come out of it'. – Participating designer

Each group were handed a unique co-creation box with mixed materials in different styles. One of the boxes featured a lot of small, colourful figurines like plastic dolls, metal toy cars and other figurative toy objects all known from children's play activities. Another box contained objects solely from nature, like pebbles, shells, woods and twigs. The third box was made of small non-defined objects in neutral colours, with inspiration from the materials of the Scandinavian design tradition like wood, metal, wool, glass and paper. To supplement the three

Figure 5.1: Designer in an internship as a child

co-creation boxes a range of different tools like scissors, glue guns, tape, etc. was available for the participants in the co-creation activity.

Children and designers worked intensively on building the life of a child with the provided materials. They had a lot of conversations throughout the activity, which offered the designers valuable insights into the children's perspective on the world, their lives, their passion and their future dreams. The process became a way for the designer to gain a more open-ended but still in-depth understanding of the children.

'We talked a lot about the life of a child and started out with the morning routines – what is happening. And then we got inspired to move on from there. And we talked about their lives and how they manage to take showers on their own while listening to music in the bathroom...'
– Participating designer

The final creations complemented this knowledge in different ways, supported by the different kinds of materials; The group who had worked with the figurative elements presented their creation in a more storytelling way – almost as a kind of puppet theatre, without that much alteration of the figures. The group with the nature-inspired box combined the different elements into an almost metaphorical dialogue where the open-ended materials took the form of whatever the children needed to express. The group with the non-defined materials used construction to build the different elements together to bring forward what they wanted to share about the life of a child. It turned out that no matter what kind of co-creation box the groups had worked with, the response from the children was the same:

'We [the children] need to have our own space, with our own rules, where we can experiment and test things in our life. A place where we are in charge and in control and can do whatever we want, without any interference from our parents and other grown-ups'. – Participating children

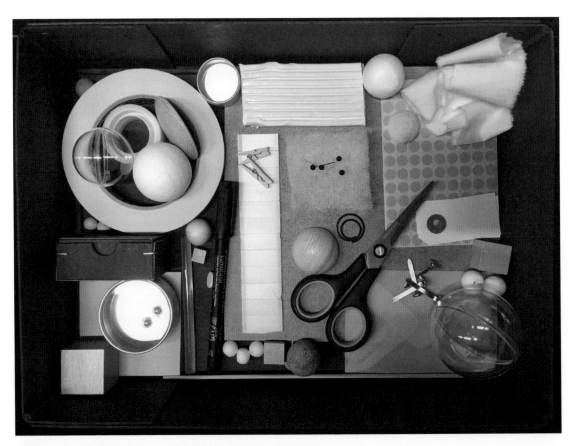

Figure 5.2: Co-creation box with open-ended materials

The case indicates that the materials are not the most important part of the co-creative method, but that the open-ended process and the specific task allowed the children to create their message through a more suitable and creative way of communicating. The designer became more of a facilitator of the explorative process than one asking specific and predefined interview question. This required the designer's ability to let go of the control and to trust the process to provide knowledge relevant for when designing for children. The designers ended with a valuable peek into how the children themselves see the life of a child – answers to questions they would never have thought of asking as a part of a regular interview.

Comparing Child-Personas

In a master's course in child-centred design for play, a group of design students were introduced to the child-centred design approach through the method of comparing child-personas with children. The method aims to confront designers with their assumptions of children (Dewey 1938/1986) by using a traditional design method; personas, but in a new and more exploratory way.

The participating children and designers were each handed out a child-persona template and divided into groups of one child and one designer. The template is inspired by a traditional persona template but modified to be understood and used by children. The children were asked to, individually and covertly, fill in the empty spaces of the child-persona template based on their own life; name, age, family members, personal interests, dreams, wishes, etc. At the same time, the designers were asked to fill out a child-persona template as well, but in the way, they expected the child would do it. This caused a lot of frustration for the designers and some argued that they couldn't do it because it would be just guesswork.

'It was really hard because you cannot easily guess their interest, what they like and so' – Participating designer

> "A humbleness toward children and the way they perceive the world is not just a suggestion but a necessity – it is the key to work with a child-centred design approach."

This frustration was a part of the process of confronting the designers with their tendency of guessing instead of knowing when designing for children – and when they work with the persona method in general. The designers got the message once again when they were asked to compare their templates with the children's child-personas, and it was obvious that that designers' answers didn't match the children's answers.

'This was also for us to know that we cannot just think we know the kids'. – Participating designer

The difference between the answers just made the children's answers even more valuable, and they gave the designers a glimpse into the life of the child. They experienced how a child's greatest wish at the same time could be to own a bakery AND to have a boyfriend, and that answers to the question on what the children think is important could range from 'brush your teeth' to 'having friends'. The designers were in general surprised on how much the children's parents, family and friends meant to them, and they realised that this was an essential insight when designing playful experiences for children.

The method of 'comparing child-personas' is not just a way to challenge the designers' assumptions on what they think they know about children or a critical remark on the use of the persona method – it is an informing way to get specific insights on children and a way to start a conversation with the child. The template can be modified to include specific questions but, at the same time, it is important that it is open and exploratory enough to capture aspects we are not aware of exists.

HOW to Design With a Child-Centred Design Approach

Designing with a child-centred design approach does not necessarily demand specific tools and methods as the ones presented in this text, but it always requires genuine respect and curiosity for the children and the context that they are a part of. This may involve a higher awareness of one's own role in the process and the ability – and willingness – to step back as a designer and let the children lead the way. A humbleness toward children and the way they perceive the world is not just a suggestion but a necessity – it is the key to work with a child-centred design approach. Not all are familiar with spending time with children or feel confident experimenting with a child-centred design approach without any pre-knowledge or guiding instruction. In that case, specific tools and methods can be applied to the child-centred design process. This can be in the form of general design methods adjusted to suit the process with children as the specific target group, or it can be predefined methods designed to obtain the children's perspective when applied to the process as the child-centred design methods presented in this text. In both ways, a great portion of humbleness is needed from the designer to be able to establish respectful and trustful interactions with the children.

'We can have so many thoughts about it beforehand, but it is just so simple... it is

Figure 5.3: Design students compare their child-personas with children

all about getting out there!' – Participating designer

Sequence of Child-Centred Design Activities

A sequence of child-centred design activities can be suggested and structured in a way that addresses the challenges and opportunities of a child-centred design approach (as illustrated in figure 4). In the beginning of a design process, when designers and children meet up for the first time, the point of departure is on 'the children's turf', i.e. their familiar surroundings, daily activities and selection of everyday objects. This is a way to make the children feel safe and comfortable with the presence of the designers. In the second activity the children

Figure 5.4: The order of the child-centred design methods from the children's turf to the designer's turf

and the designers are more on common ground, since the participating children are naturally used to creating and playing with materials, and the designers also feel more at ease based on their creative profession. The third activity moves on to the designers' turf by using an existing design tool – 'personas' – with the children. If we look at three activities together there is a systematic move from the children's turf to the designers' turf in the end.

Five Recommendations

The child-centred design approach can be accompanied by a handful of practical recommendations for entering the design process with the approach:

- Just do it – even though that you feel unprepared, having time troubles or are afraid of children
- Do it early in the process – to make sure you are actually designing with relevance for children
- Do it with children – to understand who you are designing for and the context they are a part of
- Do it through creation – to support children's creative way of communicating about their lives
- Reflect on what you do – to become aware of your opportunities in the design process

Quick Take-Aways

This chapter has through the introduction to the child-centred design approach challenged the way we are designing for children by taking the starting point in the children instead of the product. The child-centred design approach encourages designers to leave their design studios, their expert role, their predefined output and their assumptions on children, to engage in children's everyday lives for gaining an understanding of children. The presented child-centred design methods exemplify how designers can be in it together with children by taking on an internship as a child, co-creating the life of a child or comparing child-personas – all of it done together with children and on their home turf.

By working with a child-centred design approach as a designer or an innovator you dare to work with what matters – with the result of a high degree of relevancy, seen from the perspective of children. You have the potential to be at the forefront of identifying what should be a part of children's future lives, directly grounded in and linked to their related contexts. Keeping the child in the centre of attention before, during and after the development process increases thereby not only the relevancy but also the innovativeness. It opens up the opportunity for not only designing for the future but designing the future – by the use of the child-centred design approach.

Further Reading

Ackermann, E. K. (2013). Cultures of Creativity and Modes of Appropriation: From DIY (Do It Yourself) to BIIT (Be In It Together). The LEGO Foundation.

Brandt, E., Binder, T., & Sanders, E. B.-N. (2013). Tools and Techniques: Ways to engage Telling, Making and Enacting. In *J. Simonsen, & T. Robertson, Routledge International Handbook of Participatory Design.* New York: Routledge.

Dewey, J. (1938/1986). Experience & Education. In *The Educational Forum* (Vol. 50, No. 3, pp. 241-252). Taylor & Francis Group.

Feder, K. (2013). HUB for Play & Design. Kolding: Design School Kolding.

Feder, K. (2020). Exploring a child-centred Design Approach – from Tools and Methods to Approach and Mindset. Ph.D. Dissertation. Kolding: Design School Kolding.

Gunn, W., Otto, T., & Smith, R. C. (2013). *Design Anthropology.* Bloomsbury Academic.

Hart, R. A. (1992). *Children's Participation – From Tokenism to Citizenship.* Florence: Unicef – United Children's Fund.

Kolb, D. A. (1984). *Experiential Learning – Experience as the Source of Learning and Development.* Case Western Reserve University.

Pellegrini, A. (2013). *Observing Children in their Natural Worlds – A Methodological Primer.* Psychology Press.

Rinaldi, C. (2004). Staff Development in Reggio Emilia. In K. & Cesarone, *Reflections on the Reggio Emilia Approach* (pp. 62-66).

Sanders, E. B. N., & Stappers, P. J. (2014). Probes, Toolkits and Prototypes: three Approaches to making in Codesigning. *CoDesign, 10*(1), 5-14.

Schon, D. (1983). *The reflective Practitioner: How Professionals Think in Action.* New York: Basic Books.

United Nations. (1989). ohchr.org. Retrieved November 29, 2017, from United Nations Human Rights Office of the High Commissioner: http://www.ohchr.org/EN/ProfessionalInterest/Pages/CRC.aspx

Acknowledgement

I would like to thank all the participating children and designers for their engagement in the child-centred design approach – I couldn't have done this without you. Thanks!

Play Design Insight 6:

Narrative Inquiry for Play Design Opportunities

Hanne Hede Jørgensen

In this play design insight, I will demonstrate how you can do narrative inquiry as part of a play design and subsequently how to frame a play design starting with 3-to-5-year-old children's play narrative. The chapter primarily addresses pedagogues, teachers or designers who want to work with a design approach in order to co-create play cultures with young children in Early Childhood Education and Care (ECEC). Through examples, I show how a narrative inquiry approach can help you to explore what experiences, preferences and challenges young children in a local institution might have. As a quick take-away at the end of the chapter, I will unfold how you as a designer can use this narrative approach in order to promote a playful environment or co-create playful encounters with other target groups.

What is Narrative Inquiry and Why Should we do it as Part of a Play Design?

This chapter starts with a narrative approach. It is based on an understanding of human experiences as embedded in stories (Clandinin 2016). Humans grow up on stories, and stories have points of view. While we are children, we hear many stories about how to act properly, how to look, what is good and what is bad. As such, stories become a sort of cultural compass for behaving and thinking. When we tell stories about everyday life, we try to arrange our experiences and make sense of them according to this narrative compass; the narrative knowledge in our suitcases. Stories help us to create connections between relations, things, feelings, moods and identities. According to Jean Clandinin and other narrative researchers, we can say, that stories act upon us and we as humans act and think in storied ways. Narrative inquiry, therefore, aims to understand some of these stories that people tell, live and act upon. It also, however, acknowledges that when people meet, they might bring forth different stories. Meaning that the stories that you as a researcher, a designer, a teacher or a pedagogue bring with you when you make an inquiry are important because they affect your gazes, your understandings and the meanings you put into words. Narrative inquiry, therefore, ought to be a way of travelling into an open space between humans, an open space where things, identities and contexts suddenly can transform and become something new in the narrated experiences of the other.

> "While grown-ups listen to children's play stories, they might, therefore, get a glimpse into this magic world of making sense and non-sense."

In this chapter, I show how grown-ups can use this narrative approach as a gateway into the world of children´s play in order to meet the child open and curious. This means that doing narrative inquiry with children is a way of meeting the child as the unknown other. Focusing on play stories is furthermore an acknowledgement of the existential aspects of play. While playing, children create new worlds. They explore tools and artefacts and transform things, words and meanings into something else, meaning they play with sense-making, presumptions and ideas of what-if; they explore the balances between being inside play and outside, between making free choices and submitting to others, between what is good and what is bad. While grown-ups listen to children's play stories, they might, therefore, get a glimpse into this magic world of making sense and non-sense. They might hear children transform ideas of good and bad, right and wrong, normal and abnormal in a world of possibilities. The stream of creativity and folly underneath the neat surface of being a rational and serious adult can suddenly reveal itself through the play stories of children.

Another argument for using narratives as a way of interacting with young children is that telling and retelling is the most obvious form of expression to young children. Young children usually tell and show with their whole bodies what they do, experience and think. Young children do not make rational arguments for a better future. They narrate what is at stake right here and now. Telling play stories could, according to the UN Declaration of the Rights of the Child, be both a right of play (§31) and of speech (§13).

A Child's Perspective on Play

Children love to play. Being able to play with peers seems to be the main task of the day if you ask children (Corsaro 2003). Understanding play in this chapter starts with children's perspective on play and from young children's perspective play can be understood as a relational phenomenon (Bae 2009). Young children seek participation in peer culture. They want to join in. They are attracted to peers, they want to join the laughter and turmoil. Adults might interpret the

glee chorus, the fights, screams and tears as noise and conflict. It is, however, a part of the play, and when children play, they gain experience and confidentiality with the perspectives and values of other children (Pálmadóttir & Johansson 2015) as well as their own ability to express themselves within the play context. Following, adults who interact too soon in order to stop the noise or what they interpret as a conflict, risk creating obstacles in young children´s development and they might prevent the children in having some very important existential and democratic experiences.

Children, who play a lot, get much play experiences and they come to terms with many different playmates. I define these children as 'good' players, meaning they can recognise many different kinds of play and they possess the ability to find a way to join in. These children seem to thrive and grow. Not all children, however, seem to know how to enter the peer culture of play. These children cannot fully profit from other activities during the day because they use a lot of energy trying to figure out how to enter the peer group. They seem to stand outside 'the promised land', and they might need grown-ups to support them and help them to find a way to enter. How do children become good players? Maybe some of us grown-ups have forgotten what play is about. Maybe we think that we can teach children to become good players by explaining to them how to do and how not to do. Maybe we think we can support a child into play by asking the playing peers to let him or her join in.

This is not how it works in the children's world of play. To become a good player, the child has to practice play with peers and get a variety of play experiences. The child must exercise the bodily knowledge of play.

"To become a good player, the child has to practice play with peers and get a variety of play experiences. The child must exercise the bodily knowledge of play."

Pedagogues, teachers and designers should do narrative inquiry with young children in order to explore what experiences, preferences and challenges the children might have. What is presently at stake in a certain play culture? They should also do narrative inquiry for play in order to rediscover their own play skills and play challenges. Doing narrative inquiry with young children is the first step in a play design where the purpose is to support children in becoming good players. Not by explaining and teaching, but

by becoming sensitive towards the complexity of play practises in a certain group of children.

Retrieving your own Play Knowledge

As mentioned the premises for doing narrative inquiry is to understand human life as embedded in stories. Stories reveal knowledge of experiences. Professionals who work with children must be aware of two things. On one hand, their own experiences form their values and the ways they look upon children's play. On the other hand, a child's play stories include the child's knowledge and opinions on play. The first step for professionals who wants to enhance children's ability to play therefore must be to explore which stories they themselves think with and act upon. What stories do they tell? The play memory underneath is an example. I narrate it as a way of showing how play stories are embedded in culture and history, and how they can bring forth understandings of materials, relations, identities, feelings, time and space as well as the ambiguity of fun, freedom and riskiness.

Walking on Oil Barrels

'My best friend, Susan, was the daughter of the village grocery store. Sometimes when I came there, we met with the other children of the village behind the store where the oil tank for tractors stood. Here there were some empty oil barrels. When

we turned them around, we could balance on them. We could even walk upon them, rolling them. Susan was so good at doing it. So was Ken. They were both a year older than me and quite daring. When we rolled over the parking place, they soon advanced ahead of me. I had to put my foot down more often than they did. I even sometimes fell. We were whirling up in front of the store, onto the road. The hard metal of the barrels thundered over the asphalt. The sound was wonderfully daunting. Then the grown-ups came running out, scolding us for being noisy. Susan and Ken with their arms swinging to the sides rolled hastily on while I was startled and fell down. But I always came up again.

Today I would probably intervene and stop the children before they were hurt because I myself felt anxious.' (Play memory, 1970, a small village near Billund, Denmark)

In the frame of a narrative inquiry, the play experiences may reveal the storytellers' different conceptions of good and bad play, their experiences of being inside, outside or on the edge of the play, their interactions with materials, their sensations of rooms and environments, their feelings and moods regarding play, their opinions of their playmates. Play stories also reveal contextual and historical values and conceptions of play. In the story above, I narrate in order to expresses how the

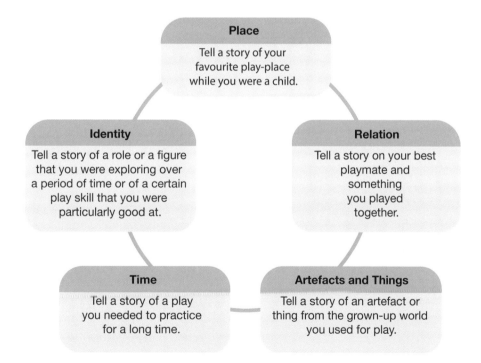

Figure 6.1: The themes are connected. You can however choose a starting point and see where it takes you

balance between struggle and freedom is the core of becoming a good player. I also, however, make a standpoint regarding children´s right to practice and fall and the role of adults. As such, the play memory reveals a polyphony of voices and perspectives on play. This is a key point of the theory of the narrative sociologist, Arthur Frank (Frank 2012). He claims that all stories are polyphone and in dialogue with different stories. Meaning when we tell stories, we do so in a dialogical sense, considering all sort of different stories that we try to make sense of. In my play memory, the story is performing a dialogue with both children´s and adults' perspective on play. I try to express the pleasure of practising play with peers by underlining the drama of building up certain play skills and keeping up with the other children. I also, however, express the perspective of an adult with a professional attitude on play culture towards other adults of today who are occupied with danger and security and who might intervene according to their own grown-up feelings of anxiety. As such, the story both try to express a child´s feeling and makes a professional point of view. This time I did so deliberately. Grown-up play stories, however, are not neutral. Therefore, you as an adult have to examine your own stories in order to understand your presumptions and more or less hidden values.

A narrative inquiry for play should as a first step frame play memories for the grown-ups who want to promote play experiences amongst children and do play design.

You can do that according to different themes. Use Figure 6.1 as an inspiration.

As a second step, you should do narrative inquiry for play with the children.

A Narrative Inquiry of Children's Play Culture

In this next part of the chapter I connect myself to a study I did a couple of years ago in a Danish Kindergarten together with other researchers, pedagogues and children (age 3–5). The study was based on narrative inquiry. We wanted to explore what type of plays the children locally preferred at this moment in their everyday life. We also wanted to investigate whether all children experienced themselves as part of the play culture in the Kindergarten. The first thing we did was frame a four-step design for exchanging play narratives:

The pedagogues went for a walk and talk inside the Kindergarten with a group of children armed with tablets. The task was that the children should take pictures of the good and the bad play places. The pedagogues, the children and I as a researcher had a gathering where children told stories about their pictures. The pedagogues and children went for another walk – this time outside on the playground of the Kindergarten. The pedagogues, the children and I had a new gathering.

This Kindergarten was situated in an old villa with two floors and many rooms of different sizes. Outside there was a large playground with a lot of trees and shrubberies. There were some routines and activities in the morning which children should attend to, apart from that children were free to decide where to play. In the afternoon, all children should play outside.

The Staircase

'The first gathering was to begin. Seeks young children sat on the floor together with a pedagogue and me. They were looking at each other´s pictures and they cheered and laughed whenever they discovered a picture of themselves. 'Look that is me and my best friend'. There were a lot of close-up pictures of the children and their friends and they immediately started to point out who was who and why they were best friends. There were also pictures of toys and certain rooms. The rough-and-tumble-room with a small cave filled with rubber balls was especially well represented in the photos and the children told us about a mermaid play that they played there. When the astonished pedagogue (who did not know the play) asked how they played this play, all children got up and jumped with their legs close together shouting: 'like a fish'. One of the children added: 'sometimes there is a shark'. Then the children jumped higher and quicker, screaming. When the children sat down again I suddenly saw that one of the pictures showed the staircase between the floors. The pedagogues saw it too and asked about the picture. Jenny said it was her picture and then she told us this: 'I love the stairs, you can climb up and down and then you can hide and jump forward'. Jenny got up from the floor and showed us how she could jump up in front of us and say 'RAAAAUGH'. The pedagogue started to laugh. While the rest of the children began to jump up and down saying 'RAAAAUGH', he explained to me, that the professionals had remarked these three little children running up and down the stairs all the time. At a recent meeting, the pedagogues had discussed whether they should block the staircase because 'We thought the three children could not decide where to play. We even discussed if the children were having trouble joining the Kindergarten play community and regarding their wellbeing and development in general. Now she tells us, the stairs are the play'.'

As mentioned at the beginning of the chapter, we open up spaces between us and bring forth new perspectives on things, relations and identities, when we make a narrative inquiry. We suddenly understand that the world is sometimes not what it seems and that we always can understand differently.

Figure 6.2: The stairway and play room

When it comes to young children, play stories are essential because play is the core of meaning to children. Most children seek inclusion in the play culture with peers. Friends matters to even very young children. In the story above, we see that the children get excited about seeing themselves with their friends in the pictures. We also see that the children start joining in on the playful conversation by using their bodies and voices to express themselves in the same ways that their peers. This joint expression of jumping like a fish or saying RAAAAUGH might be a way for children to recognise and practice the core of these plays. We can interpret the situation above as an arena for exchanging play stories, but moreover – because of the way young children use their bodies while communicating – we can interpret the situation as a setting for doing play practice together. It

becomes clear that the professional gets new knowledge on the children´s play culture in the Kindergarten right now as different than he thought it was. It also becomes clear that when professionals frame this kind of narrative settings, they promote the children's opportunities to express and practice play together. In the example above, the children get the opportunity to express together how to do a mermaid and a staircase play.

Following, professionals should support and frame narrative inquiry of play stories for three reasons. First, as a way to support all children – also the children who do not usually tell much – to express themselves about their everyday life. Second, they should do so in order to frame joint play practices for a group of children. Third, they should do so in order to create a play design that considers what kind of play children actually play. By doing so, the professionals might support all children's ability to participate in an actual and local play culture. In addition, professionals can make design for play in order to challenge the play culture of the Kindergarten. In order to do so, you need to know what play preferences the children already have.

Looking for Play Design Opportunities in Natural Environments

Doing narrative inquiry for play design is a way to make young children participate in the making of the play culture in a Kindergarten. As such, the idea of the design derives from the democratic preoccupation of Participatory Design and includes both practical knowledge and research knowledge of how to work with children´s perspectives. Rather than being occupied with creating and describing new plays, you should focus on what is actually happening in the Kindergarten and amongst the children and pedagogues when you come up with a new play design. You can do so through prototyping new play arenas in order to see in what way a certain prototype affect the players, their relations and play practices. Prototyping as such is a way of facilitating new presumptions and possibilities (Marcus 2014). Meaning that when you change the frames of children's play, something most

certainly will happen and this something will affect your understandings of the children. Therefore, you might see new possibilities. Finally, I link the narrative inquiry for play design to theories of social design. The core of social design in my understanding is together with the participants in a fellowship or an organisation locally to promote and create social changes. As mentioned, the purpose, in this case, is to support children to get access, to join and to participate in a play culture. The purpose is also to challenge the play cultures so that children constantly get opportunities to 'move on' within play and involve themselves in new adventures and practice new play skills.

Following is a play design starting from the mermaid story. The design operates with the 'items': mermaid stories, things, freedom of choices for children, places and the role of the professionals. These items are at play when the pedagogues frame new arenas of mermaid play in a play design that takes a variety of play opportunities into account. The design seeks to be open-ended, meaning the pedagogues do not create fixed settings. They aim to keep following the children, trying to be explorative in order to get further knowledge of the children and the play culture in this particular institution – knowledge that might become a starting point of new play design.

Examples of Play Activities Initiated by Pedagogues

There is a Storytelling activity where one of the pedagogues each Friday together with children tell and dramatize mermaid stories. Children are divided into two groups across ages. All children attend this activity.

In the cellar, there is a workshop where children can make mermaids and sharks out of cardboard and clay. A pedagogue is there to help and give advice. This activity is a free choice. Children could join if they wanted.

In a small room in the attic, the pedagogues and children create a water mood room with blue walls, pale and flickering light and sounds of water, here is a lot of pillows and portable rubber shapes. In this room, the pedagogues might not enter. In here is free play and the children can join as they please.

In the kitchen, there is a 'mermaid'-gastronomy activity each Tuesday and Thursday. Together, children and pedagogues explore what mermaids might eat and then they make and eat it. Children are divided into two groups, 3-4 years and 5 years. All children attend this activity.

In the playground, one of the pedagogues creates a 'swim-from-the-shark'-play. The pedagogue is the shark. The children can join if they want.

In the playground, one of the pedagogues together with the eldest children, build a boat out of old wooden boxes, hammers and nails. The purpose of the boat could be to hunt sharks or to go on mermaid expeditions. The children can, however, use the boat as they please.

Narrative Inquiry for Play Designers

This chapter primarily addresses pedagogues, teachers or designer who wants to work with a design approach in order to co-create play cultures with children. The design approach is not a didactic approach. A narrative design for play is an explorative approach. The professionals cannot teach children how to play. Starting from children's perspectives they can, however, enhance opportunities for children to practice play together. They should do so in order for the children to express themselves and in order to become more experienced players.

For designers who want to frame a play design with other target groups than young children, this chapter is relevant as it offers ideas of how to do a narrative inquiry as part of a field study before and during designing for play. Such an explorative field study is essential to designers. I will emphasise the polyphony of stories. It is crucial for designers who want to work narratively to keep in mind that stories are dialogical, they express points of view and they do not always correspond with our own stories. At the same time stories work on you, they affect you somehow, and you might even get annoyed or surprised when you hear stories that differ from your own. As such, a narrative approach is also investigating your own presumptions and values if you chose to listen to how and why they affect you. This is important knowledge in co-creation setups.

Within the frame of participatory design, the question of co-creation and collaboration with other people, situated in other contexts than the designer, is a core issue. This chapter offers an understanding of how humans think and act within narratives and how designers can use these cultural and personal play stories in order to explore what matters locally and frame a co-creation setting or a play design. This might be relevant if you want to design encounters with elderly people, for example. Many elderly people might not remember all aspect of the present, but they do probably remember their play stories and they might be quite willing to join a playful setting in order to co-create atmosphere and dive into the past together with other elderly people or with younger people or children. You could also consider a narrative inquiry approach if you aim to do a design in order to promote a gay and playful culture in the nursing home or in a hospital. You could explore what artefacts or places were at the core of the play stories and design new rooms or surroundings according to this.

Another target group, with whom the narrative inquiry is a very applicable approach, is refugees or foreigners in general. In this case, you must be very careful to frame the narrative setting in a way where you give as many narratives as you aim to get. This is an ethical question of meetings on equal terms. At the same time – and for the same reasons – you must make sure to frame the settings with a sharp focus on the 'good' play experiences. You might even add to the folly and gaiety in order to co-create an atmosphere that could be a relaxing break from the traumas of reality here and now. At the same time, you might explore a cultural perspective on humour and childhood. The knowledge that you get from your narrative inquiry, you can use in order to design encounters with refugees and non-refugees or in order to design rooms in the surroundings of a refugee camp or a language school that might offer a playful atmosphere.

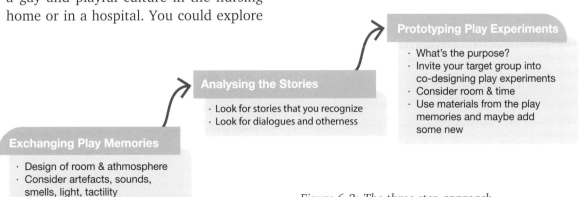

Prototyping Play Experiments
· What's the purpose?
· Invite your target group into co-designing play experiments
· Consider room & time
· Use materials from the play memories and maybe add some new

Analysing the Stories
· Look for stories that you recognize
· Look for dialogues and otherness

Exchanging Play Memories
· Design of room & athmosphere
· Consider artefacts, sounds, smells, light, tactility

Figure 6.3: The three-step approach

Quick Take-Aways

A narrative design for play for designers has three steps as illustrated in Figure 6.3.

The first step is to consider how 'the other' perceives the world of play. Children, elderly people or refugees are maybe obvious others, but you might also think about target groups closer to you and open up to their perceptions of the world. It might be another than you thought it was. Formulating and investigation play memories with other people ought also to be a way to explore the designer´s own play experiences. In this part of the design, framing settings for exchanging play memories is the core. Think of the atmosphere and think of how to get started. You can use artefacts or pictures, but be aware of that these items – if chosen by you – might narrow down the associations.

The second step is to explore the play stories that you collect. Including your own. What are the stories expressing? What seems to matter for the people whom you, the designer, wants to involve further in the design? What kind of dialogues can you detect? In this part of the design, the designer can analyse the stories, following the five themes from Figure 6.1. Focus on artefacts and tings, identities, relations, places and time.

The third step is together with your target group to make prototypes of play experiments starting from your analyses of the narratives. The purpose could be to enhance atmosphere, mood and culture or to frame playful encounters. Prototyping play experiments starting from the narrative inquiry is an explorative design. You should do so in order to gain new knowledge through the design. You can choose to include one of the five themes from your analyses or you can try to involve all five of them in different set-ups.

Further Reading

Bae, B. (2009). Children's Right to Participate- Challenges in Everyday Interactions. *European Early Childhood Education Research Journal*, 17(3), 391–406.

Clandinin, D. J. (2016). Engaging in narrative Inquiries with Children and Youth. New York, NY: Routledge.

Corsaro, W. A. (2003). *"We're Friends, right?": inside Kids' Culture*. Washington, D.C.: Joseph Henry Press.

Frank, A. W. (2012). Letting Stories Breathe – a Socio-narratology. Chicago: The University of Chicago Press.

Marcus, G. (2014). Prototyping and Contemporary Anthropological Experiments with Ethnographic Method. *Journal of Cultural Economy,* 7(4), 399–410.

Pálmadóttir, H. & Johansson, E. M. (2015). Young Children's Communication and Expression of Values during Play Sessions in Preschool. *Early Years: An International Journal of Research and Development*, 35(3), 289–302.

Acknowledgement

The Researchproject mentioned were done together with Anette Boye Koch, Hanne Laursen & Pia Rauff Krøyer, VIA University College, Aarhus, DK.

Play Design Insight 7:

Expressions of Play as a Resource for Creative Idea Generation

Antonia Clasina Södergren

This Play Design insight invites you to explore how moments of ended play still can inspire new playful design experimentation. It is also about play as source of inspiration to become creative again which might enhance well-being in a busy life and add some bliss of play between the 'to-do's'.

Pre-schoolers' particular play behaviour have inspired three techniques that might re-connect you with playful experimentation. These techniques create an experimental framework that assist you to explore and analyse structures, activities and materials in a deeper level than you usually might consider. You start to see play's expressive interactions everywhere and ... it might unlock playful ideas.

Introduction

To create something adds bliss of play between the 'to-do's'. It is significant for everyone's wellbeing to engage in activities that are spontaneous, free of schedule and provide enjoyment. It is within playful activities that you can experience a personal free space, relief from stress, pressure or difficult situations as you can express yourselves in manners you like, arrange your activities how you wish or play with materials in ways you prefer.

You might have come across a particular urge to create something, desiring to get exciting ideas or have faced situations where it would have been great to have some. But, you might also have felt limited by your current state of skills, lack of time or narrow experience. You might not be sure what, where or how you are looking for to tap into the rather mystical grail for creativity and get ideas to spire. Or maybe you would like to arrange a workshop to initiate playful creative activity and stir design ideas by making participants aware that they actually can be creative – no matter how far out that may seem for some. Or you might be interested to receive some tools to activate children, youngsters or teens in creative, hands-on playful processes to obtain ideas and get them curious for the world beyond the digital worlds offered by their iPhone. Or you would like to find ways to engage creatively together with children or foster ideas for playthings for them in a relatively scarce amount of (family) time. It could also be that you are in contact with elderly, children with special needs or others for whom you wish to create a playful experience *for* or *with* to let them connect with their 'inner self' and play.

The section below aims to add some bliss of play to explore solutions for these suggested areas of interest. It offers you some easy steps accessible to everyone, everywhere. These steps explore one particular form of play which can link everyone to idea-generating activities. The only 'devices' you – as a play design researcher – need are your body, learning to see with your eyes and hands; a mobile phone and a notebook accompanied by a pen.

> "Expressive interactions are those interactions that leave a sign of activity in their surrounding environment."

The particular contribution to play design is that the following pages present techniques for designers and non-designers alike to distinguish various expressions of play interaction and use them as a source for creative idea generation. These expressions are space-bound, yet not necessarily time-bound. The techniques can make expressive interactions that are gone worth looking at one more time and sharpen your attention while expressive interactions are still taking place. Hopefully, it will raise your awareness to see and explore the entanglement of play in materials, environment or in human interactions. This might inspire you to get new ideas or perspectives on play. At the same time, this might connect you in a deeper way to the playful exploration of your surrounding environment for your own or others' interests.

Play Interpreted as Accompanied by Expressive Interactions

Play is like laughter – composed by many things, released across generations, though highly individual, and still not necessarily bound to a particular time or space. It occurs both logically and unexpectedly at the same time. Play can be experienced in different ways, since play is, in real life, very dynamic and multidimensional in a complex world.

Expressions of play can be spontaneous or planned to create a contact with and path for an *exchange* between the inside (cognitive perception, imagination) of an individual with the outside environment (material, environment, other individuals). This exchange is expressed by a creating shape (i.e. drawing, building), a sound (i.e. music, utterances) or bodily expression (i.e. movement), amongst other possible expressions. These ex-

pressions can be experienced by everyone through his/ her sensory apparatus (vision, hearing, smell, taste and touch). Almost everyone can experience the joint dynamics of expression and exchange happening within (play) interactions with materials, humans or other things present in the surrounding environment as these expressions are perceived, for example, by eye-sight, touch or hearing.

Throughout this chapter, the term play is used to define a play perspective that interprets play as a dynamic enjoyable activity accompanied by various *expressive interactions*. Here, enjoyment is more than just laughter. Enjoyment can be expressed by having a particular direction of attention and focus shown in entire body position, body limbs activity and the involved sensory apparatus (i.e. eyes). Yet, it can also be detected by smiles and spontaneous utterances in combination with this particular absorption in an activity causing various expressions.

Expressive interactions are those interactions that leave a sign of activity in their surrounding environment. Everybody is able to leave these signs of activity, regardless of skills or experience. This interpretation of play points at the issue that there resides the potential for idea generation and designing for both designers and non-designers in having a closer look upon those experienceable 'signs of activity' that are expressions of play interactions.

Often, when people want to involve other people in design processes and creative idea generation, they arrange activities and materials in such a way that they have 'signs of activities' as results. These expressions of play interaction provide insights concerning the participants' experience of the process, provide grounds for ideas and might indicate the next step to explore an issue more precisely.

The sections below focus on how signs of play activity can be a source for creative idea generation. As you explore in practice these signs of activity and their entanglement with materials, environment or in human interactions it might stir your ideas.

Construction Play as an Example of Expressive Interaction

One form of expressive interaction that might connect you in a deeper way with playful exploration is construction play. It reveals imaginative play and can easily be distinguished, while it at the same time might further explain what expressive interactions are and how these can serve as sources of inspiration.

Notably, seen in figure 7.2., constructions look quite similar across age groups. Except that adults can implement more trained skills within their constructions. This insight is underlined by the following figure 7.3. The results of a paper-tape experiment with

Figure 7.1: Seen in the pictures on the right, construction play can be practiced by pre-schoolers alone, together and is not bound to particular material, combinations or space.

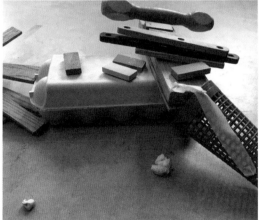

adult designers compared to pre-schooler results show that skills actually have significance in producing expressive interactions. Yet, the results of adults (left) and the results of pre-schoolers (right), show both 'signs of activity' regardless particular skills or experience.

So, despite varying skill levels, the creative potential residing within these pre-schoolers can come to expression. This is shown in three examples in the subsequent figure 7.4, where pre-schoolers constructions might due to its symbolic expressiveness i.e. provide a new idea for emballaging products, suggest different playground designs or could inspire architectural work.

In this chapter, construction play practices are simply defined as 'a tactile play activity producing constructions', since construction play leaves tangible witnesses of play activity. Constructions are defined as any 'tangible, three-dimensional shapes composed of a variety of tangible materials. Often resulting in abstract and expressive forms' (Södergren & Mechelen 2019). Construction play practices can be an inspiring form of play interaction since it produces visible expressions of play that reveal in itself both aspects of its creation process and the result of 'the making'. Seen in Figures 7.1 to 7.4, these visible expressions display in themselves visual structures, hint towards activities to obtain these structures and show selected materials. The visible evidence of this play activity points at one particular advantage. This form of expressive interaction

Figure 7.2: Comparing the result of an adults' construction (bottom picture) to those created by pre-schoolers (above): it does not look significantly different.

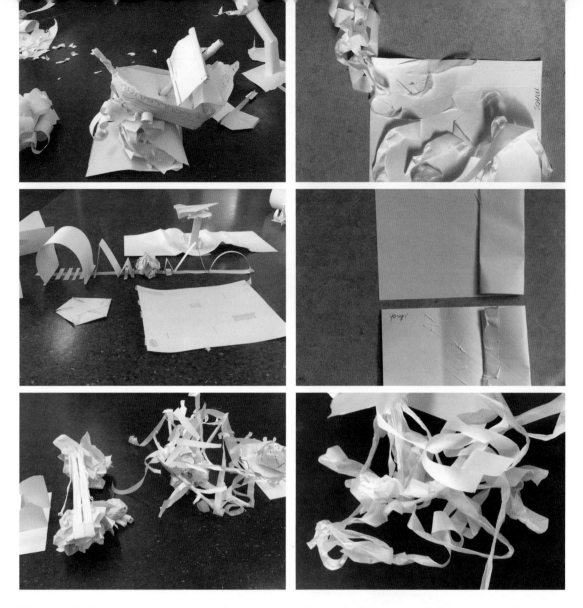

Figure 7.3: Same experiment, with the same material and the same task in the same language. Pictures on the left are adult designers' constructions; pictures on the right are by pre-schoolers aged 3–6.

can effortlessly be captured by mobile devices taking photos, video or even audio recordings. Another advantage is: all age-groups – including adults – can approach it and accomplish it.

Building further on these matters, the following 3 techniques invite you to change your ways of experimentation – maybe even play with a different sense of awareness that releases a different sense of exploration or even imagination.

Central to the first technique entitled *ViT-C* and the last technique called *LevelXplore* is the main emphasis to show

Figure 7.4: Constructions might inspire new ideas for emballaging, playthings for playgrounds or architectural work.

you how you can notice expressive interactions and turn these into insights concerning play experiences, playful experimentation or even unlock your own ideas. Ideas can be achieved since they both show a step-by-step structure yet still leave space for creative, spontaneous experimentation. The second technique, 'play- punctum', sharpens your overall attention to the composition of expressive interactions evolving from the particular moments of enjoyment in play behaviour.

1. ViT-C method – Moments of Tangible Engagement Inspiring (Play) Design

ViT-C (Visual Interaction Tactile-Construction) technique focuses on the previously described 'expression of play interaction': construction play. It provides practical steps for finding constructions in your surrounding environment and shows you how to use those expressions of interaction as a practical guide to design your own ideas. More precisely, ViT-C focuses on finding and photographing constructions discovered in your surrounding environment to initiate designs for play. The ViT-C technique is a design process composed of a model and two constraints. The constraints are a chosen theme and some aspects of a (play) design that you would like to integrate into your result. The ViT-C model sets an overall focus of attention for you, whereas the constraints challenge you to

Figure 7.5: Shows examples of moments of tangible engagement left behind by its creators.

explore your chosen theme and design in more detail than you usually would. These constraints assist you in maintaining focus while exploring constructions without limiting the flexibility of your approach. Before demonstrating the practical application of the ViT-C technique, the following text will introduce the three-fold components of the ViT-C technique – the model and the two constraints.

Background Knowledge of ViT-C

If you are attentive, you can discover that people leave tangible memorials of a particular moment of engagement seen in Figure 7.5.

As you can see, these moments of tangible engagement are represented in constructions that are visible and tangible. Past expressive interaction can be seen in various objects or structures left somewhere – displaying an individual's absorption within a process of doing and thinking before they left that particular spot. If you have a closer look at Figure 7.5, you might even see that it is possible to reflect upon the limb movements (i.e. finger, hands, feet, entire body) that created these structures or the combination of materials on top of the hay, sand or grass areas. These tangible witnesses of past activity seem to carry a performative notion in a particular space as they can still communicate the story of their creation to you. And it is exactly here, the ViT-C technique helps you to reflect upon its 'story' and use it as inspiration for ideas.

The ViT-C – Technique in General

Preliminary research results amongst pre-schoolers showed, that there are three matters in construction play practices that impact the focus and intensity of engagement with materials. These are implemented in the ViT-C model seen in Figure 7.6 in order to direct your attention to analysing constructions in a particular manner.

First, you explore the tactile qualities. You can ask yourself questions like i.e. does the construction show different sur-

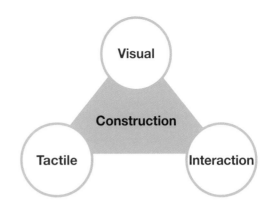

Figure 7.6: The ViT-C model

faces, what are the things which make it interesting to 'the touch' and why?

Second, you explore the visual qualities. What materials do you see, and what are the possible qualities of the material

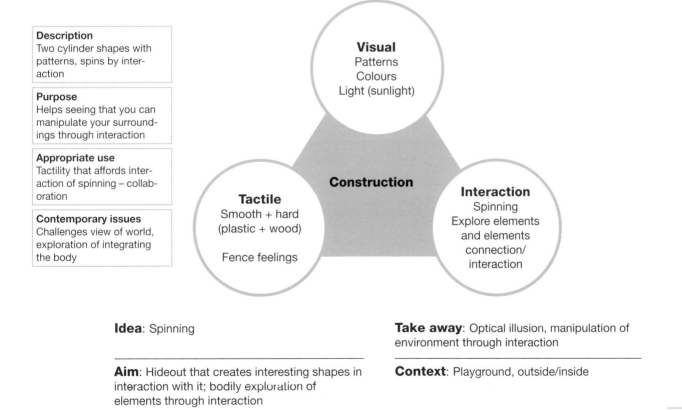

Description
Two cylinder shapes with patterns, spins by interaction

Purpose
Helps seeing that you can manipulate your surroundings through interaction

Appropriate use
Tactility that affords interaction of spinning – collaboration

Contemporary issues
Challenges view of world, exploration of integrating the body

Visual
Patterns
Colours
Light (sunlight)

Construction

Tactile
Smooth + hard
(plastic + wood)

Fence feelings

Interaction
Spinning
Explore elements and elements connection/ interaction

Idea: Spinning

Take away: Optical illusion, manipulation of environment through interaction

Aim: Hideout that creates interesting shapes in interaction with it; bodily exploration of elements through interaction

Context: Playground, outside/inside

123

Figure 7.7: Shows the application of the ViT-C model by design students (see details next pages).

attracting your eye that might impact your interaction?

Third, you explore the possible activities that created this construction. The 'i' in the name ViT-C, pinpoints at the crucial aspect of interaction (i.e. bodily engagement) during a 'making' process, since it links the visual and tactile aspects, so a construction actually can appear. How more diversity in materials, how more diversity in visual and tactile aspects and consequently more interaction possibilities to explore.

Two Constraints –
Theme and Play Design

Two particular aspects set the constraints for this method. First, a theme. Choose a theme within expressive play interactions that has relevance for the people or the environment you want to design an idea for. Describe why it is relevant to you. Second, find a (play) design that appeals to you in its tactile and visual qualities as well as and interaction possibilities. It helps you to have some visual idea in mind to illustrate where you want to go with your idea. Describe why it is relevant to you.

Student Example –
Application of ViT-C

Master students in Design for Play from Design School Kolding Design applied the ViT-C technique during only two workshop days. This might encourage you to try out this technique which can be done in a limited amount of time. The students were given a brief description of a theme and a play design that aimed to stir ideas into directions that connect well with pre-schoolers behaviour and their construction play practices. The students had the possibility to explore the provided play designs physically to stimulate idea generation. In addition, they received a step-by-step description of the ViT-C-process.

Figure 7.8: Fröbel's gifts

124

Figure 7.9: a. Boy creating a hideout   *b. Girl Playing in her 'secret place'*

Constraint 1: Theme – Hideouts

It is possible to distinguish one particular theme significant for pre-schoolers' play and wellbeing: hideouts. The freedom of allowing adults and children to discover and create private worlds in the world plays a role in self-exploration. Hideouts invite reflection and activities that connect the inner and outer being. It often seems to carry the notion of a private sanctuary where individual imagination can unfold differently – out of sight. Yet, sometimes 'guests' are invited to explore

that secret place together which enrich the total experience of the hideout.

Constraint 2: Play Design – Design a Gift Similar to Friedrich Fröbel's Gifts

In connection with construction play practices, architect and designer Friedrich Fröbel (1782–1852) had a significant influence on perspectives of pre-schoolers' play.

Seen previously in Figure 7.8, Fröbel's designs are signified by a simplistic, generic

and multi-applicable design. He labelled them 'gifts', which is still in use today. His gifts activate the senses and allow various cognitive development exercises. He applied three tenets when he designed his gifts: unity, respect and play (Manning 2005), which are still relevant design principles (i.e. expressed within democratic design). Therefore, this play thing sets the constraint to design something that contains simplicity, is generic and multi-applicable. Figure 7.11 shows a quick overview of one possible application of the ViT-C process completed by the Design for Play Master students, whereas the How-to box to the right shows you the process in practical steps.

Figure 7.10: Sequence of inner-outer exchange surrounding the play-punctum. It expresses enjoyment, clear direction of attention and focus displaying that relations exist between the observer, the expressive interaction and its creator. See details next section.

How-to – the Exact ViT-C Process
Design a gift to create hideouts

1. Decide upon a theme you want and have a picture of a design that resembles some features you would like to have in your idea.
2. Take photos of tangible moments of engagement at a playground or any other site
3. Choose one visible feature (i.e. structure, colour, combination of different materials) that is interesting to you.
4. Choose one tacit feature (i.e. surface-structure, material quality) that is interesting to you.
5. Distinguish the possible interactions/movements (i.e. drawing, scratching, stamping) and limbs involved (i.e. hands, fingers, nails etc.) causing the construction you photographed. Choose an interaction or a sequence of interactions that is interesting to you.
6. Sketch different ideas by a clustering and create a collage of photos. Then, design your idea that.
   a) has the theme hide-outs, b) includes the 3 choosen aspects found in your photography, and
   c) is a gift similar to Fröbel.

3 ASPECTS THAT INSPIRED OUR DESIGN

VISIBLE
PATTERNS
COLOURS
LIGHT
SUNLIGHT

TACTILE
SMOOTH
HARD
PLASTIC
WOOD
FENCE FEELING

INTERACTION
SPINNING
EXPLORE ELEMENTS
CONNECTION
INTERACTION

EXAMPLES OF SKETCHING & PROTOTYPING

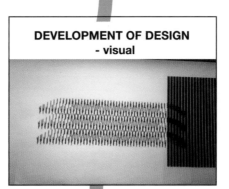

TACTILE VISUAL INTERACTION

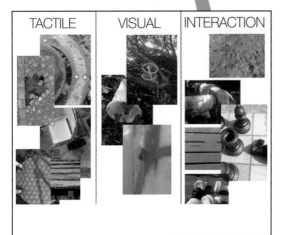

"OUR GIFT"

DEVELOPMENT OF DESIGN
- visual

MOOD BOARD:
Photographs of tangible moments

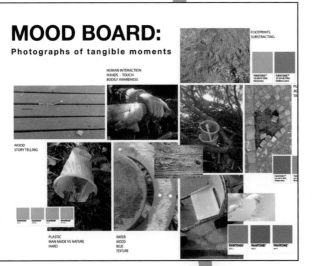

DEVELOPMENT OF DESIGN
- tactile - interaction

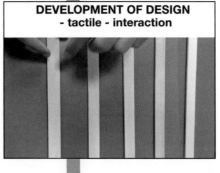

YOUR GIFT

2. Play-Punctum – a Moment of Play Captured by Photography as Inspiration for (Play) Design

The 'play-punctum' sharpens your overall attention to the composition of expressive interactions evolving from the particular moments of enjoyment in play behaviour. It enables you to have a closer look at photography and video recording material. It might also inspire you to find more specific features and qualities residing in expressive interactions that could inspire you to experiment with new (play) design ideas. This might give you different ideas how to design a 'thing', a material or an environment that is composed by features, qualities or variables that might give a great experience of play by consciously addressing the dynamics of collision, fusion or confrontation in its design.

"Awareness for the 'play-punctum' will assist you in analysing 'what is' activated and 'with whom' that causes enjoyment in the experience of play."

What is 'Play-Punctum'?

Awareness for the 'play-punctum' will assist you in analysing 'what is' activated and 'with whom' that causes enjoyment in the experience of play. In line with the previous description of expressive interactions, the play-punctum describes more precisely the moment within an expressive (play), where the 'exchange' between

How-to 'Play-Punctum'

1. Find and film a playful interaction around an object, environment or a situation you want to explore. 5 up to 10 min.
2. Make screenshots from the video recording-in 10 second intervals or less. As it makes sense to you. Print the series of pictures out.
3. Choose 10 pictures where you see most enjoyment expressed.
4. Look at each picture and write notes according to figure 9.
5. Choose the picture where you detect highest enjoyment after 4. Try to write down qualities, features and other components of that play-punctum (i.e. tactile, visual, etc). Do these features cause fushion, collision or confrontation?
6. Explore the chosen play-punctum from 5. Within its interaction process. Look at the other pictures and note what happened before and after to explain the appearance of play punctum.

Picture	Describe interaction that you see – What are the body parts doing exactly?	Describe focus of attention – position of the body	Describe focus of attention – direction of the eyes	Are there interesting experiences of touch? (tactile)	Are there interesting visual experiences?	Is there any stimulation from other individuals in the same environment?	Is there any stimulation from other 'things' in the same environment?	Do you see a particular spot, a 'thing' or activity in the environment that centres attention of individuals in the room?
Time:								
Picture 1								
Time:								
Picture 2								
Time:								
Picture 3								
Time:								
Picture 4								
Time:								
Picture 5								
Time:								
Picture 6								
Time:								
Picture 7								
Time:								
Picture 8								
Time:								
Picture 9								
Time:								
Picture 10								

Figure 7.12: Table for play-punctum notes

the inside (cognitive perception, imagination) of an individual with the outside environment (material, environment, other individuals) happens. This moment of exchange evokes enjoyment, a particular 'direction of attention' and 'focus' seen in Figure 7.10 previously.

The experience of the play-punctum depends on 'where' in the process the moment of inner-outer exchange happens (with what kind of materials, etc.), 'how' (what intensity level, the composition of variables in the room), and who 'else' is present. However, the play-punctum is not specific and is inter-twined in a sequence of play interactions, relations and embedded in a process as time goes. Yet, with the play-punctum technique, you are able to nail down the impact of different variables in an interaction process more precisely. Attentiveness towards the 'play-punctum' also allows you to find particular 'centres of play behaviour' in a particular room or environment.

Concluding, it depends on the type of inner-outer exchange happening in a play-punctum if it is experienced as re-creative and positive play or evokes other forms of play like destructive play, rebellious play (Leeuwen & Gielen 2018) or even dark play (Mortensen, Linderoth and Brown 2015).

3. LevelXplore – Material Exploration within Play Activity as Inspiration for (Play) Design

Expressive interactions are often accompanied by materials enabling that expression. Therefore, it is crucial to be aware of the impact and range of possibilities a material has. Materials incorporated in designs impact behaviour and activities. In connection with idea generation, awareness of this dynamic enables you to explore what material qualities are engaging and consequently integrate it in your (design) ideas or creative activities for others. The LevelXplore technique contains easy steps accessible for everyone to discover that, by playful interaction with material, you can actually get ideas. It invites you to try out a material exploration process based on the pre-schoolers' playful process of performing it during play.

Accordingly, the LevelXplore technique seen in the 'how-to box' can be viewed both in its separate levels of exploration as well as in its holistic dynamical process. During any interaction, materials can be explored on level one to four, by jumping back and forth or materials can even get exchanged. This technique will equip you – after some practice- with a more detailed comprehension of materials and their impact on interaction. It enables you to observe yourself or others at these levels within any interaction-process and trains you to enhance your own or others level of material exploration, experimentation and seeing.

How-to 'LevelXplore'

Level 1
You notice its presence. You see the material, have a definition in mind 'what it is' and do no further interact with it.

Level 2
Tactical exploration: *'what it is'*. You explore a chosen material through diverse activities as you i.e. twist, turn, stretch the material. This is accompanied by activating in different ways your senses to experience the material. You i.e. listen to its sound, perceive it colours in different conditions and touch surface structures. At this level you might even experiment with particular features or qualities of the material in more detail. Here, note if you either jump to level 1, stay at level 2 or move to level 3 during your exploration.

Level 3
Function exploration: *'what it can do'*. Based on your knowledge of level 2 *'what it is'*, you explore your chosen material further in order to find possible functions for it. Here, you can combine various diverse materials and objects to explore different options and effects. Here, note if you jump back to level 1 or 2, change material or why this particular material invites you to explore it more.

Level 4
Constructions exploration: *'what it can become'*. Here, you can try out various ways of creating constructions with this material in combination with other materials. Just choose whatever other materials you find around you to create at least 5 different constructions. It might be a challenge to not experiment with a *'what it should be'* or what is it *like'* in mind. Try to allow *'what might be's'*, it might result in a interesting and surprising (design) idea direction rather than risking the creation of a cognitive barrier.

Conclusion

Hopefully, this chapter has shown you a practical path for what, where and how expressive interactions during play can occur as a resource for (design) experimentation, so you can start your own creative idea generation processes for yourself or others. The more you learn to distinguish various expressions of play interaction, the more you can use them as sources for creating the bliss of play between the 'to-do's'. This might, in fact, inspire you to approach your 'to-do's' from a different perspective and... maybe more playful.

Quick Take-Aways

Key attention in this approach can be given to the following issues:

1. Learn to distinguish expressions of play within artefacts, activities or within human-interaction, so you can pinpoint the possible causes of expression, the means of expression and how these expressions can possibly provide you some guidelines to get playful ideas yourself.
2. See what principles actually stir play enjoyment, so you can integrate those as principles in your ideas.
3. Experiment at any time – try to find a material, structure or environment to explore.
4. Be present, forget your schedule for an hour and give time to experiment. Let materials grow on you and play with different ways of structuring them, viewing them and try out what is possible with it.
5. Close your eyes and touch – in various ways a great variety of materials to re-kindle sensitivity to the differences of 'feel'.
6. Pursue to experience materials, structures or environments that challenges your senses to explore connections between body, perception and reason.

Further Reading

Leeuwen, van, L. & Gielen, M. (2018). Design for Rebellious Play. In: L. Magalhães and J. Goldstein (Eds.), *Toys and Communication. Palgrave Macmillan*, London.

Manning, J.P. (2005). Rediscovering Froebel: A Call to RE-examine his Life & Gifts. *Early Childhood Education Journal*, Vol. 32, No. 6, June 2005.

Mortensen, T.E., Linderoth, J. & Brown, A.ML. (2015). *The Dark Side of Game Play. Controversial Issues in Playful Environments*. Routledge.

Södergren, A. & Mechelen, M. (2019). Towards a Child-led Design Process A Pilot Study: when pre-schoolers' play becomes designing. *IDC'19 Conference proceedings*, pp. 629-634.

Acknowledgement

With kind permission of DSKD MA design for Play students Bethany Rose Coggins, Randy, K. Heath, Karen Juhl Petersen and Sigrid Vinther Hansen, their 'students design process' got integrated. Thank you!

MA students at TU Delft, spring 2019, NED, for their paper-tape-creations. Thank you as well!

Thanks to all who are part of Designbørnehuset *Sanseslottet*.

Play Design Insight 8:

Designing for Play in Youth-based Educational Situations

Line Gad Christiansen

In this chapter, I will present ways of using elements from play as tools for enhancing the motivation for learning for young people. The tools can be used at any scale, but I would always argue to apply as much from play as possible. This chapter is mainly aimed at those working with young people in high schools, college or higher education, for instance, but the tools can also be used in design in general, as some of them have arisen from that context.

Introduction

Do you know this experience? You have prepared for a course-topic, put effort into making it interesting, the slides have small visual details – especially that small animation with cats and dogs, that state your point about differences. You start the lecture, and your pupils (which are from now on referred to as learners) try to pay attention... except for that one person, who always has to go to the toilet right after the break or who has an important phone call in the middle of class. After ten minutes, four more have lost focus on your teaching, and their phones, computer, looking out the window or doodling have suddenly caught their attention instead. Twenty minutes into class, there are only those two girls who actually take notes and ask questions. The rest have mentally evaporated from the room and, for the rest of the lecture, you are annoyed about all the effort you have put into nothing – but hey! At least you have met the requirements for the course.

I know that the example above is the extreme version; exercises, group work and small breaks often help shift that situation. But over and over again, I have seen this tendency, both with children, adolescents and adults. I have taught at many different school levels, from children up to university, and they all have a certain expectation of how teaching should be: someone (an 'expert') standing, talking and showing slides, while the learners sit quietly and ask questions – though often they don't. I have made it my mission to try to change that expectation, and in trying to do so, I have experimented with different small and large interventions in class. Some worked well but demanded too much compared to the outcome, some did not work at all, and then there were some tools and interventions that just worked. In this chapter, I will present some that worked across different contexts; therefore, this chapter consists of practical lessons learned from a variety of educational situations.

This chapter aims to present different tools and approaches to the teaching situation, but it does not deal with explicitly formalised learning outcomes found in curriculums. Instead, it shows how to use play-design to increase didactics and motivation. What will be presented is not the only way, nor a 'one-size-fits-all', so I strongly encourage you to harness what makes sense to you in this chapter, give it a try and make it your own – you know your learners best.

Play as a Driver for Motivation

For this chapter, I use play as a driver for motivation through engagement, ownership and social bonds. As Stuart Brown (2012) stated, play is closely associated with social bonding, creativity and innovation. There are advantages to playing; even just a little bit on a regular basis will still contribute to a greater feeling of happiness and being able to act on problems or turn them upside down. Play is involvement in activities where motivation and

> " There are advantages to playing; even just a little bit on a regular basis will still contribute to a greater feeling of happiness and being able to act on problems or turn them upside down. "

freedom can exist; it is doing that activity without a need for a certain outcome, as the activity often will drift dependent on catalysators from objects and/or other people. What do I mean by catalysators? I'll use this example:

Maya and Marie are playing with dolls. They have named their dolls, given them each a persona, dressed them and now the dolls are drinking tea with Maya and Marie, with that nice tea-set Marie got for Christmas. Suddenly Justin, Marie's little brother, comes in and asks if he can play with them... 'No, he can't! He doesn't have a doll, he just has action figures and teddy bears, and none of them can drink tea'. Marie and Justin's mother intervenes and states that they must include Justin in their play, and they forcefully accept.

'Then we can just play dad, mom and baby: Justin you are the baby, come and lie here. Then we said that the baby slept, while the mom and dad drank tea'.

The dolls and the tea-set are catalysators for a certain play-activity; though they can be used in many different ways (the dolls could disagree and use the tea-set as weapons), it invites a specific interaction. Justin changes the playing field, and they have to negotiate a new play-activity that includes him, taking the point of departure in the play activity they are already involved in.

Problem-based
Learning and Playful Learning

When we are playing, we are active members of that activity – otherwise, it is not really play (Brown 2009; Zosh et al. 2017). In other words, playing enables us to keep focus and be actively engaged in that activity, though the activity might shift in nature quite often as seen in the example with Marie and Maya. In connection to the educational setting, playful learning has hence arisen. Playful learning can be explained by the example of Coding Pirates in Denmark: in extracurricular activities, learners can participate in workshops where they through exploration and creative ideas of creating certain small robots or using existing play products such as *LEGO Mindstorm* and *LittleBits*, for example, in an attempt to build and code solutions to achieve their goal or idea. This is done with supervision and guidance from people within the field of technology, so it is driven by motivation and curiosity within a framed environment.

In the following sections, I present aspects and tools to consider when you want to increase your learner's motivation through playful activities. I will touch upon problem-based learning as a potential for facilitating play through teaching; safe spaces will be presented as it is both a prerequisite and an outcome when using play as a tool, and I will present aspects of play and design that relate to learning. Through these three parts, I aim to propose simple ways to increase motivation in educational situations.

One approach that I find to be useful to combine with play elements is *problem-based learning*, which provides ownership and exploration. Problem-based learning gives the learners the chance to really take their learning into own hands, by defining and working with a problem-based focus. The combination of using different tools and approaches tends to create a space where you as the teacher and the learners have more equal stakes in the learning. One way of doing this, as mentioned, is problem-based learning, where the learners are working on projects with topics and problems, through a given frame (by you). They get to choose

what they would like to work on within the frame, and through a structured and guided way, finding the information they need, process it appropriately and conclude on it, for example, by:

- Finding the information: Google, articles, books, interviews, observation or something sixth
- Processing the information: categorising, finding insights, doing analysis, etc.
- Conclude on it: prototyping, sketching, summarising, etc.

This takes elements from the design but in a simplified way. If you want to expand it further, I would suggest you have a look at a design model and the methods for that, e.g. double diamond or the 6C model (Friis 2016).

While doing problem-based learning, you could let your learners do presentations with peer input often through the process, use mindset activities, use play elements and then, of course, combine it with short lectures. What often happens (not always, and sometimes only for part of the process), is that the learners take ownership over their learning. I have even done whole classes based on two large and three or four smaller problem-based projects, with a maximum fifteen-minute lecture each time. My students have asked me 'when are we supposed to learn something?', they tend to associate the courses with something good: They do voluntary

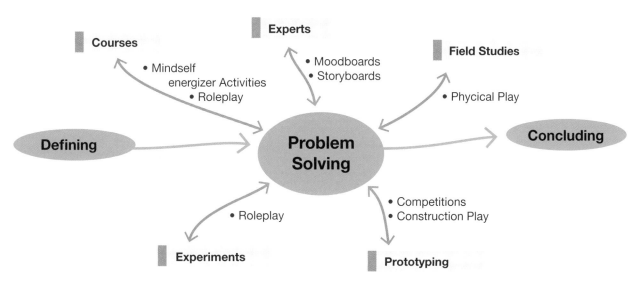

Figure 8.1: A combination of problem-based learning play elements

homework, they understand (most of) the material better, rates of practising and attendance are higher than the classes where I haven't dared to go through. The important points to take from this are that you need to define problem areas or topics that the learners can choose from and you then guide the learning process through their projects.

For example, I had a class that was hesitant towards databases and information technology, which were the topics we were going to cover. So, I gave them a challenge: Decide on a problem that you (in groups) would like to work on, with one of the following requirements in mind: creating a game, designing a webpage or making an app. They decided on different things, e.g. one group wanted to make a game that was based on safe sex (I think they were testing me on this one); one group wanted to make an app

that made laundry easier when moving away from your parents; another group wanted to create a website for a bakery that one from the group worked for. I then guided them through different tools available (the goal for me was never to create something complete and nice, but more for the learners to work with technology and databases in a more exploratory way). At some point, I did a fifteen-minute lecture on the possibilities of databases and gave them the challenge to incorporate a database to their solution in a meaningful way, which they did, with various success, but they all did it and put effort into it.

I guided them and chose when they were ready for the next challenge within the projects they were working on and then exploited that they had already invested time and thoughts in their projects when presenting something that the learners perceived as boring. It wasn't as boring to figure out a way to save all the bread-types in the webpage, to define different sexually transmitted diseases and the

---

---

safe choices to avoid them, or to categorise the signs and meanings of laundry as 'just making a database', as these tasks had purpose and additional meaning to them.

Three Ways to Create Safe Ludic Spaces

One aspect that I have found is important to consider when using a playful approach towards teaching is the safe space that is created. When ensuring that the space is safe (which can be physical rooms, the mental space of not feeling exposed unnecessarily, not having too high demands compared to competencies, etc.), you set the stage for play to happen. Through play, new safe spaces can occur, e.g. socially between a group of people who have not been comfortable around each other, the safe space of daring to speak up in class even if you are not sure what you are going to say is correct, or not letting mistakes defeat or define you.

The Relationship between Expert and Novice

The room where the learners are supposed to receive their learning must be one where they feel that they can ask freely, involve themselves in play activities without judgement and where you as the facilitator or teacher try to remove some of the social insecurity that many learners have. My mentor, many years ago, told me that when he had new learners, he deliberately had small typos in his slides, to decrease the perception his learners tended to have: that he was perfect. I try to communicate to my learners both what I know and a few examples of what I do not know, also to decrease the difference between me and them; when guiding them, I often use the phrase 'you are the expert in you'. It seems cliché, but it works. Regardless of the way you approach this, just remember to think about how to create a space where your learners feel safe to express themselves, as this will increase their learning outcome.

Groups, Pairs and making that safe

Another aspect of creating safe spaces is when you pair or group your learners, it again should be in a safe way. If the learner already feels exposed before the activity, the benefit of that activity will not be as high. One option is that you can pair people up by focusing on them finding someone in the room who has the same or opposite feature (shoes, hair length, coloured shirt, etc.). Focus on features that are neutral in a social setting. Then, if a person has not been chosen, it is not because nobody wanted to pair up with him/her, it is merely because this person has a unique type of shoes on that day, and then you – as the teacher – can pair the last couples up. If you need groups of four, for example, then just do a similar exercise but now in the pairs they have already created. Or in more long-term group work, you might want to use another approach. There are then different ways of doing it, but again: whatever you decide to do, base it on the most neutral aspects possible, e.g. their passion for a specific topic, speed-dating, team-roles that they have defined individually (For instance *Belbin's Team Roles* – see Belbin 2012) or letting them write ideas of what they would like to work on and then put the ideas in categories that define groups or pairs.

Break it up

The last suggestion I have to ensure a safe space is to break shifts up as much as possible. If you say to your learners: 'now we are going to do something different, come out to the floor, and let's play', what often happen is that their minds will jump ahead: they will start thinking 'I would rather stay seated', 'I am not in the mood for playing right now' and so on. Some will jump to an excited state of mind, but others will jump to this more negative state, which will result in you experiencing reluctance towards what you ask of your learners (we all do this, it is a natural thing for us to try to analyse what is to come and then prepare for the necessary reaction towards it). As we are inclined to seek each other's confirmation, you are additionally at risk of the negative reaction spreading.

So how could you do so? By breaking the shift up in as small parts as possible, start with getting the attention 'I want you all to look up', the next steps could be: 'empty your hands (wait a bit), stand up (let them stand), come out to the floor (wait until they are all out on the floor), find someone who has the same eye colour as you' and so on. By doing so, you control the focus, and you aren't allowing for peoples' minds to jump to a state based on what they think will happen. This will make it easier for you to get your learners involved in what you ask them to do, as when they first have moved to the floor, the reluctance towards the activity and the need for sitting down and hide behind a screen, book, table, etc. will decrease for a while.

Play As a Vehicle for a Prepared Mindset

Some of the playful activities I have found that work well are aimed at preparing us for the next challenge, meaning that the activities focus or enable a required mindset in the participants. We use this quite a lot in design to guide the participants towards a desired state of mind. If you want your learners to start opening up or thinking creatively, the activities must be of the same nature. One example could be pairing your class up and asking them to walk around in the room. When they focus on an object, they must ask the other person what the opposite of that object is, for instance, 'what is the opposite of a window?' The other person then tries to answer and explain why (there are no right or wrong answers), and then they switch turns. This little activity fosters creative thoughts, and then an idea generation session, brainstorm, input to a topic, etc. often tend to be more approachable. If your learners need to start making decisions, find activities that are of that nature. If you want your learners to speak up, do activities that require everyone to speak; they are much more inclined to do so afterwards, too. Remember that no matter which activities you decide on, they should be within the safe space, so don't ask your learners to speak up about something they might be shy about or put them in situations that will make them feel uncomfortable, as they would take it with them to the next activity. What I have presented here is a way to implement small activities that do not require much time, often around five minutes or so, to do. They are useful tools for you to have in your backpack, both as planned activities, but also in case your learners lose focus during the day.

Roleplaying and Scenarios

A bit more time and planning are required when using games or more elaborate playful activities. Surprisingly enough, I've found that roleplaying scenarios based on a course topic also tend to engage the learners, even to a degree where they forget their breaks, not wanting to stop the activity.

I had a class of 16–17-year-old learners who were supposed to learn about technology and ethics, so I set up following scenario (You can find many similar scenarios, there is no need to define your own):

· Setting the stage: You are all in a courtroom (see Figure 8.2), trying to figure out who was a fault after an incident where an autonomous car had driven slowly into another car that had misjudged how fast it could get out on the road from a sideway. The autonomous car had gotten new tyres earlier that week, and it turns out they were changed to the wrong size, so the computer in the car miscalculated. Is the mechanic, the 'driver' or the driver of the other car at fault?

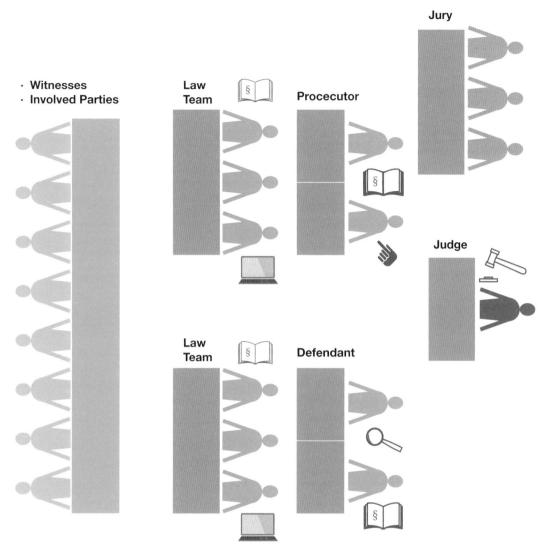

Figure 8.2: Court room – roleplay and scenario example

- Defining the roles: I gave each group/ pair a role: a judge, two lawyers, the three involved parties, a jury.
- Ground rules: I set up some ground rules and made a schedule determining when they were in court (2–3 times) and when they should prepare with arguments, find rules and regulations, etc.
- Failsafe: Finally, I stated that whenever I said 'stop', they had to stop the activity and focus on me (to ensure that I had a way of stopping them if the activity became too personal).

What happened was that they accepted this roleplay to a degree, where they used their break to call mechanics and other experts to find good arguments. We ended the roleplay with a discussion and reflection on a broader level. The learners took ownership and enjoyed the activity, and for the exams almost a year later, they still remembered even small details about this.

Besides the example above with roleplay, you could also think about using physical play, construction play or gameplay as drivers for the learners to get engaged with the topic you want to teach.

· Roleplay, for instance creating scenarios with actors, defining and shifting group roles, or the use of storyboards and cartoons.
· Physical play, such as geocaching, taking images of specific objects in the surroundings, treasure hunts, trying it out (e.g. climb the tree if you want to understand why others do it).
· Construction play could be using LEGO Mindstorms and similar, creating a physical version of a problem (think in different materials: clay, cardboard, etc.), breaking something apart and building it up again, tinkering with materials or objects.
· And lastly, gameplay, e.g. by creating own board games based on a topic or problem, competitions with rules and winners, using existing games to play out scenarios or by breaking down old games and creating something new.

Using competition can enhance the motivational drivers in learning. I planned a competition combined with construction play using LEGO Mindstorms when wanting to teach about block-coding (see Figure 8.3): I divided the class into groups, created a field with obstacles on the floor with tape and physical objects, presented a timeline and requirements (the robot must be able to either move, lift or shove an object on the field) and gave clear guidelines on how to win, which, in this case, was based on three aspects: the design/idea, how the robot dealt with the obstacle, and how it navigated through the field. I supervised during the competition every time a group got stuck, but overall, the learners found solutions on their own, which seemed to motivate them even further.

To teach another group of learners about historical buildings located in the city-area of the school we were in, I used a combination of treasure hunt and geocaching: The learners were handed a map with the start and end, and through geolocations and hints about the (next) specific building, the learners found their way around the city and tried to place as many of the locations as possible, starting with the first X on the map and ending with the other X on the map, but using the hints and geolocations to find buildings in between. They were given a time in which they had to be back, presented with a point system, and sent on their way in groups supplied with their phones, a map and a notebook.

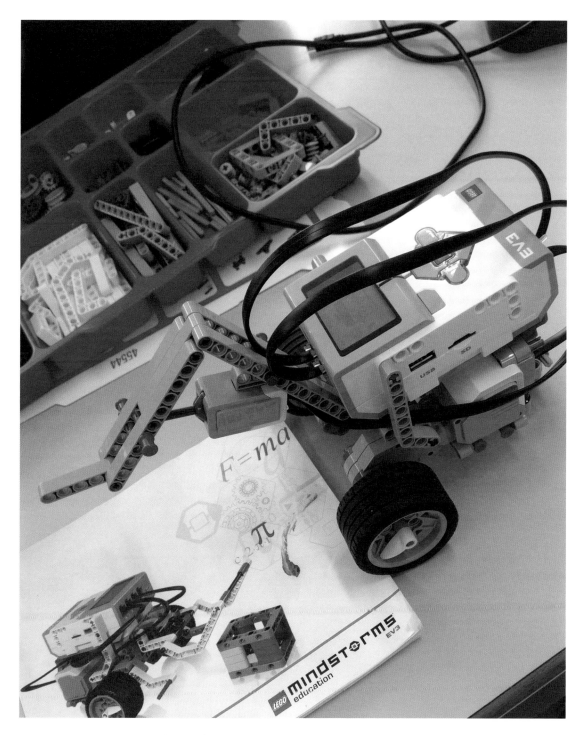

Figure 8.3: Construction play with LEGO Mindstorms

Quick Take-Aways

In this chapter, you were presented with three overall approaches: (1) Play problem-based learning, (2) Cultivate save ludic spaces, and (3) Roleplaying and scenarios – which you can use either on their own or together. Using playful activities can – but I would argue should not – be a seldom occurring thing you use. If you decide to apply some of these ways I have presented above, either directly or redefined into your own versions, and they work, try to use them regularly in some way. Just remember that you will need to change between the type of activity a bit over time; otherwise, the playful aspects are at risk of decreasing or becoming routine, reducing the strong effects. Benefitting from being playful requires practices in being so. Not everything has to be the full play experience for the benefits to come – small elements here and there in the everyday educational setting can be enough – but you and your learners will crave more!

Further Reading

Belbin, R. M. (2012). Team Roles at Work. Routledge.

Brown, S. (2009). *Play: How it Shapes the Brain, Opens the Imagination and Invigorates the Soul.* London, England: Penguin Books, Ltd.

Friis, S. A. K. (2016). The 6C Model: the Contribution of Design to open, complex, Problem Solving. *The International Journal of Design in Society,* 10 (3), 11-31.

Zosh, J. M., Hopkins, E. J., Jensen, H., Liu, C., Neale, D., Hirsch-Pasek, K., Solis, S. L. & Whitebread, D. (2017). *Learning Through Play: a review of the evidence.* LEGO Foundation, DK.

Acknowledgement

To all the students I have tested ideas and playful activities on and who have played along with me, thank you. This includes, but are not limited to, my former EUX- and HHX-students in Soenderborg, the pupils and teachers I worked with from Aadal-school in Esbjerg, the students from Aalborg University Esbjerg and the students at the Designschool in Kolding. A special thank you to Mikael Weide Jensen.

Play Design Insight 9:

Designing for Playful Citizenship

Mathias Poulsen

In this chapter, I propose that to engage in social play is also to practice democratic participation, fostering a special kind of 'playful citizenship'. I address the widespread issue in relation to a number of contemporary societies and communities, where many citizens feel disconnected from and frustrated by representative democracy. To do that, I focus on events as an arena where such play can happen, and I develop a template for play events. By the end, you will be ready to start designing your own play event to encourage playful, democratic participation.

Introduction

'Two people dressing up in cardboard armour to engage in a not-so-deadly fight in the middle of a library'.

'Strangers dancing passionately in public, exchanging smiles and laughter, their bodies interacting in surprising ways'.

'Professionals who get so immersed in building figures out of Play-doh and other simple materials that they forget what they were doing'.

'Small figures drawn with chalk on the street, inviting passers-by to see their environment through a different lens'.

'Students mustering the courage to be present, to engage with unknown ways of interacting, and to show vulnerability in a university setting'.

These activities are all examples of people – strangers – who, sometimes against all odds, have accepted an invitation to a play event, to open up, be present and to play sincerely with each other. I will argue that through such sincere, playful encounters that take place in civil society, we all have the ability to cultivate a much more vibrant *everyday democracy,* opening a greater variety of possible futures.

Framing the Chapter

This chapter is for anyone who wants to bring people together for play events and experiences with the potential to foster increased democratic empowerment. Whether you work in public institutions or private companies is less important, as I see the need to strengthen democratic participation everywhere, in both formal and more informal settings.

What I will describe is less of an operational guide or manual, and more of a prism through which to see play as a form of democratic participation. I suggest that the prism can be applied to *any* design practice or event by critically questioning the potential for a democratic play practice *anywhere:*

· as an analytical tool to critically examine the democratic potential of an existing event or experience, or
· as a design tool to expand the space for democratic participation in existing events or experiences or to design a brand-new event or experience.

Revitalising Democracy

Though democracies are still celebrated around the world as an exemplary form of government, we are also witnessing a deep crisis of democracy, where trust in democratic institutions is declining. If democracy is to survive, we need to revitalise and reconfigure what it means to be a democratic citizen.

Which images does the word 'democracy' conjure up in your mind? In my experience, it is quite likely that you're thinking about presidents and prime ministers, national elections and televised debates, ripe with shouting and hostility, parliamentary negotiations, winning majorities and so on – in short: all the trappings of *representative* democracy, which we can call 'big democracy'.

> " The core idea in designing for playful citizenship is to create opportunities for people to engage in sincere, playful exchanges of dreams and desires. "

Big events like elections may be the grand spectacles of democracy, yet they tend to overshadow something potentially more important: *everyday democracy*. In my eyes, it is exactly in our everyday life in civil society that democracy truly comes alive through the ongoing, vital encounters between ordinary citizens. This is where we negotiate the conditions for the lives we share. Let's call this 'small democracy'.

By shifting focus from big to small, from the formal to the more informal dimension of democracy, we create new opportunities for participation, reminding us that we *all* have civic agency. For the remainder of this chapter, I will be talking about the 'small democracy', exploring how play events can be seen as an arena for democratic participation.

The Politics of Play

Contemporary democracies have been described as devolving into the so-called 'politics of necessity' and a 'de-politicisation' where politics has become a mere issue of managing the established order, a domain reserved for experts (Mouffe 2018). This leaves us with little room to explore alternative political approaches and possible futures at the level of 'big democracy'.

While many would likely consider play an innocent endeavour devoid of and detached from politics (and maybe even from reality itself), I contend that the opposite is true: play is always *already* political, and 'play is not detached from the world; it lives and thrives in the world' (Sicart 2014). Just like design, play is political because it makes statements about how we might live together. Play is political when it resists instrumentalisation, demonstrating how an activity can have value with no measurable outcome; play is political when it transcends the contemporary focus on the individual, connecting people and cultivating communities; and play is political when it insists that our lives and the world can always be different.

Play is, in the words of play scholar Thomas S. Henricks (2015), a 'social laboratory':

'When people agree on the terms of their engagement with one another and collectively bring those little worlds into being, they effectively create models for living'.

Such engagement can be seen as a unique form of democratic practice that is imbued with immense vitality and curiosity, where we can boldly imagine radically different worlds.

Designing for Playful Citizenship

The core idea in designing for playful citizenship is to create opportunities for people to engage in sincere, playful exchanges of dreams and desires: who they wish to be and how they want to live (together). These profound exchanges are rarely the results of long thought processes or conversations, but instead, they simply emerge through acts of play.

When I design for this kind of play, I have but one goal in mind: to create the conditions for play to flourish. Quite often, we are expected to deliver certain outcomes and while this can indeed be worthwhile, it should never be in the foreground *when* we play. In my experience, this is

almost certain to lead to disappointment and frustration, as we see our intention to design for play get hijacked by other agendas – be it citizenship, learning, motivation, creativity or similar.

I suggest that we can design for a better version of democracy, but I do so because I believe this will, in turn, improve the conditions for play to flourish further. Maybe the purpose of democracy is simply to create societies where people are safe and secure enough – to play?

Events and Communities of Play

Designing for play can take many forms: from physical toys and objects, playgrounds, amusement parks and installations over digital games to events and other more ephemeral experiences. While all of these can foster civic agency, in my own work, I have focused primarily on designing *play events* – designed *for* and *with* the *play community*.

An event can be understood as 'intensive environment-making' with the 'potential to transform the various partaking actors' (Refslund & Knudsen 2014). I usually prefer bringing people together in physical space, and I am particularly interested in seeing events as connected, linking them together to foster a sense of continuity. While a single event can be deeply meaningful, it is when events are tied together, allowing people to build familiarity and relationships, that communities can be formed and grow over time.

I founded the international play festival *CounterPlay* (see: www.counterplay.org) in 2014 to create a forum for a serious, dedicated, interdisciplinary and playful investigation of play. In what I consider a form of radical co-design, it was developed as a framework for playful participation, where a play community could emerge and actively contribute to shaping the festival, ideally experiencing a deep sense of ownership and responsibility.

Through the Prism of Play

In the following, I will draw on my experiences from CounterPlay and describe a prism based on three dimensions of play that I have seen resonate particularly well with democratic everyday practices:

· Playful Participation
· Embodied Deliberation
· The Playful Imaginary

Playful Participation

Many scholars of democracy have argued that civic participation is declining along with our trust in democratic institutions (Runciman 2018). Italian social science professor Donatella della Porta (2013) argued that the 'quality of decisions could be expected to decline with the decline in participation, as the habit of delegating tends to make citizens not only more apathetic but also more cynical and selfish', and she continues by stating that participation is 'praised as a school of democracy: capable of constructing good citizens through interaction and empowerment'.

This is where play comes in, as play is participatory by nature, making 'people aware of their capacities for social agency' (Henricks 2015). In play, 'open dialogue is important; so is respect, commitment to the group, and egalitarianism' (Henricks 2016). When I consider play as vital to democracy, it is precisely because play is inherently participatory, creating

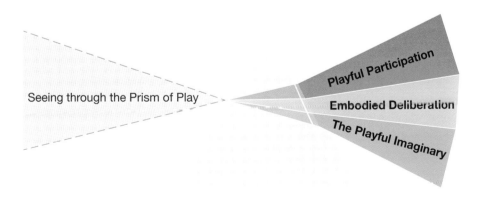

Figure 9.1: Through the prism of play

Figure 9.2: Playful participation

a wide range of opportunities for practising our social agency, while reinforcing the feeling that our decisions and actions actually matter. In a profound play experience, we don't doubt our agency, and we realise that we can have real power to influence the course of the encounter. This kind of participation often raises a series of questions as it challenges the established order of things, demanding that power and agency must be distributed amongst everyone playing.

Example One

In designing for playful citizenship, the intention is to celebrate the agency of the players rather than enforce a certain way of applying the design. This is the ethos of CounterPlay. When organising the festival, we always stress the importance of participation throughout. Before we decide on the theme for each festival, we engage in lengthy conversations with our play community, and the same is true when we prepare our 'call for proposals', which is written in open, shared documents. When people arrive at the festival, we repeat this message over and over:

'Remember that the more you participate, the more you put yourself into play, the more you will bring home with you. The festival should inspire you to be active; to be present in the moment; to let your guard down and open up to the other participants and to new thoughts and ideas; to take yourself less seriously; to set your imagination free; to dare to be joyful and hopeful'.

This approach is a double-edged sword, and people coming to the festival for the first time are often surprised by the amount of responsibility we place on their shoulders. That can be overwhelming, as most of us are more used to attend events where we 'lean back' and remain at a safe distance from the action. However, almost all of our participants eventually step up to contribute actively. This is seen in small incidents, where people share their voice to suggest new play activities or ideas, as well as in larger events that transform the festival as a whole, both of which demonstrate a sense of ownership and agency. That step is rarely taken because we encourage it, rather it is moments of play that empower people to suddenly embrace their responsibility and agency.

At one of our earliest festivals, a participant came up to the stage immediately after I had welcomed everyone, and she asked me if it wasn't about time we started playing. I could only agree with her, but I had not planned an activity, so I just gave her the stage and the responsibility to get everyone to play. We have not started the festival without a shared play experience since.

These demonstrations of agency also sometimes reach out of the festival itself, such as when a few participants established the 'Re(p)lay Box' (See: https://playreplaybox.wordpress.com/) to extend the play experience. Or when a participant suggested that we should publish something together, and we made a proper book (see: Poulsen et al. 2017) that was entirely based on contributions from the community.

Embodied Deliberation

When was the last time your body acted democratically? In my experience, our physicality is rarely considered relevant for democratic participation (apart from when we take to the streets – demonstrations depend on mobilising bodies). On the contrary, there is a longstanding tradition to perceive the political as being based on rational deliberation, from the famous Greek philosophers to Habermas. Here, deliberation is commonly understood as conversations between like-minded, critically thinking people (mostly men). By reducing deliberation to rational conversation, we maintain the conception that our bodies have no relevant contribution to make.

Again, play is different. Play creates a space where a different kind of deliberation or 'quality strife' is possible (Skovbjerg 2016), one that aims to extend and enrich the play experience rather than make it collapse in fruitless conflict. In this encounter, the Habermasian notion of deliberative democracy is expanded, allowing for a more inclusive, participatory approach, where deliberation takes place not only through rational discourse, but also embodied interaction. When we play really well, we set our bodies free and they contribute massively to the experience, but we don't think about it or care much about what other people think. Whether we are playing football, skipping rope, hiding and seeking, play-fighting, climbing trees, dressing up or dancing, we allow our bodies to figure prominently in the meaning-making process. The way we physically navigate a room, interact and maybe touch other bodies is part of exploring and negotiating ways of being together.

Perhaps because we usually reduce our bodies to vessels for our brains, they can be sources of great joy and vitality. When we play, our bodies can act in ways we are not familiar with and they can surprise us when they lead us to new places or enter into exciting postures. This often leads to shared laughter and an embrace of that which may seem silly at first. Much energy and many fresh perspectives are hiding in silliness, however, if we dare to transgress the notion that bodies have to behave in certain ways.

Example Two
At CounterPlay, playful movement is everywhere, and people are not necessarily talking a lot but allowing their bodies to express how they feel, who they are and what they can or want to do. This is made even more evident when we see people with different physical capabilities insist on creating a space for all these bodies to co-exist together, engaging in activities that allow everyone to play a meaningful part.

One of the more familiar forms of embodied deliberation can be seen when people dance with each other. We always include at least a couple of dance sessions, where it is not about making the correct moves or looking good but simply about experimenting with embodied interaction and communication. We have also realised that if you bring a live band to play a concert in the morning, many people will instinctively start dancing, and suddenly their bodies are 'negotiating' the space in a wholly different way.

The festival takes place in a public library, Dokk1, and we are always eager to explore what is and is not possible in such a space. What happens, for instance, when

Figure 9.3: Embodied deliberation

you move around like a flock of birds, walking slowly, then jumping, running, sliding along the floor, gently touching the surfaces you encounter? Or when you are suddenly not only allowed but actively encouraged to crawl all over the chairs in a conference room? Or when two people decide to dress up in cardboard armour and engage in a dramatic fight in the middle of the library?

At some point, members of our community developed a concept called 'Power-

Point karaoke', where slide decks would randomly be assigned to a group of presenters, who would have to improvise their entire presentation on the spot. One 'presenter' then decided that her Power-Point presentation was made up of three people, who would change their stance once an imaginary remote was clicked. This was hilariously silly, and it certainly created a space for a unique kind of embodied deliberation.

The Playful Imaginary

If the current crisis of democracy is indeed a crisis of participation, it seems likely that this is in turn caused by a crisis of imagination. We have apparently been unable to adequately reimagine a set of democratic participatory practices that are meaningful in contemporary society.

Whereas our collective democratic imaginary seems severely challenged, the playful mind suffers no such inhibitions. Play allows us to 'imagine and experience situations we have never encountered before' (Brown 2009 p. 34) as players 'de-stabilise their own understandings and inhabit new circumstances' (Henricks 2016). Immersed in play, we effortlessly imagine entirely different worlds along with new ways of interacting and living.

Example Three
'CounterPlay is one of the few public events that brings together people from widely divergent disciplines, and yet are united by their devotion to making the world a little more playful. Bringing them together like this, to play and talk and share each other's vision, creates an unforgettably playful, creative and productive environment and helps all of them to find a larger and more inclusive perspective on their work'. – Bernie DeKoven

When strangers meet at CounterPlay, they eagerly imagine and insist on play as a legitimate form of co-existence for

Figure 9.4: Playful imaginary

adults. Since the beginning, we have framed the festival as a micro-cosmos of an alternative 'playful society', where we could play together to explore other ways of learning, working and living together. Through conversations, shared reflections and especially through play, a different world is imagined, where people are less bound by familiar conventions, traditions and habits. This is perhaps the most important reason why so many participants claim that they feel safe and 'at home' because play is setting everyone free to pursue whatever they can imagine.

We encourage such an explorative approach right from the onset when we invite and select the contributions for the festival programme, and we try to maintain this spirit in our online community. As both a literal and metaphorical way of reimagining what is possible, we invited our participants at CounterPlay '19 to create a 'kaleidoscope name tag' as the first activity when they arrived. This was meant to inspire everyone to see the event – and the world – in a different light.

Also, at CounterPlay '19, artist Lucy Read did a performance called 'Playing at the edge of the bed', where she invited participants to join her in a bed to 'cosy up and reflect, let off steam and jump, bring your lunch for a picnic and using the pillows and bedsheets as your canvas, draw, or write your thoughts to create a collaborative artwork'.

> "If the current crisis of democracy is indeed a crisis of participation, it seems likely that this is in turn caused by a crisis of imagination."

Another even-more substantial consequence can be seen when we occasionally have participants who begin to reimagine their lives. Over the years, it has happened several times that people inform me that attending CounterPlay helped set them on a new trajectory in life.

Play Event Design Template

Pulling together the themes I have laid out in this chapter, I propose a simple template for designing events where new conceptions of playful citizenship might emerge. It should not be considered an instructional manual with all the answers, but rather a set of flexible guidelines.

Play Event Template

This template can be used to design your first play event to foster democratic participation. It should not be considered an instructional manual, but a set of flexible guidelines or stepping stones that can be tailored to your specific event.

	Event Title	Organiser	Purpose
Before Event	**Time Frame** How long is the event? How is time divided between activities?	**Participants** How many people will come? Who are they?	What is the purpose of your event? For you? For your participants?
	Setting What does the venue look like? How does it support the event?	**Materials** Do you need specific materials? Where will you get them?	**Safety by Design** What will you do to make people feel safe enough to play?

	Framing	The Play Session	Reflection
During Event	How do you frame the experience for the participants?	What kind of play activities will you present to explore: • Playful participation • Embodied deliberation • The playful imaginary	How will you help people to reflect on the play experience?

Figure 9.5: Play event design template

Safety by Design

We try to design for events and play experiences that push boundaries, question what can be said and done, transporting us outside of what is usually considered possible. When it comes to the notion of playful citizenship, this is the very purpose: to reimagine how we might live together through the act of playing. As the democratic potential of play is only ever realised when people are truly present, dare to show who they are, sharing their hopes and dreams, the experience has to be deep and sincere. If it is shallow, it will not matter much.

This is neither possible nor responsible to do unless the safety of the players has been given sufficient attention in the design process. While there is a longstanding and important discussion about *physical risk* in the design of playgrounds and play equipment, I am more concerned here with *psychological safety*. Will whomever we invite to play feel safe enough to open up, be truly present and set themselves free to play?

It may be relatively easy for someone like me to design for what makes *me* feel safe, but that is a woefully inadequate approach. I'm a white, able-bodied man and designing to make people like me feel safe would be the most effective way of excluding everyone who is *not* like me. After all, this is what (white) men have been doing for millennia, and for democ-racy to thrive, we need more equality and far greater diversity, rather than reinforcing the structures of patriarchy. It is advisable to do thorough research, improving your understanding of the needs and dreams of others, but to truly represent their perspectives on the world, you have to involve them in a process of proper co-design. You have to do your very best beforehand, and then pay careful attention to the people engaging with your experience as it unfolds.

In Advance

Depending on the space available and the play activities you want to include in the event, it may require some practical setup beforehand.

- How many people will attend?
- What is the time frame?
- Which age group(s) will be represented?
- What are the space requirements: indoors or outdoors? Open or closed? Size?
- Do you need certain materials? Objects?

These are some of the questions we always ask in advance. In the following, I use a fairly short play event of two-to-three hours as an example. It can be both shorter and much longer.

Framing the Experience (Time: 15–30 minutes)

Framing and setting the scene is very important, with a special attention on building trust and fostering a sense of psychological safety. In some situations, you may wish to describe the framing of the event as an experiment in democratic participation, but this is not always the case. It is a delicate balance because you don't want participants to focus too hard on expected outcomes – such as civic agency – *while* they play.

The Play Session
(Time: 60–120 minutes)
This is the core of the experience, where participants (hopefully) get deeply immersed in play. There are no rules or limits to the kind of play activities that can take place, so long as it builds on the three cornerstones to foster democratic participation:

· Playful Participation
· Embodied Deliberation
· The Playful Imaginary

While it can be any form of play, we have seen good results with open-ended formats that support a high degree of movement and physical interaction. We often involve construction using simple materials such as cardboard, but also draw heavily on role play, imaginative play and traditional forms of play and 'folk games'.

Reflecting on Play
(Time: 30–60 minutes)
One of the qualities of play is that we tend to forget about time and space, becoming deeply immersed in the play experience. It is exactly when this happens that play can be most profound, fostering a sense of safety, which again encourages people to be present and sincere in the moment.

Despite the immense value of being deep in the play experience, there is a simultaneous need for a reflective practice in connection with it. This sometimes leads to a paradox, where we want people to let go, to dive deep, but we *also* want them to pay attention, be aware and reflect upon the experience.

While we insist that reflection is important, we often fail to provide sufficient opportunities for this at CounterPlay. More to the point, perhaps, we regularly fail to demonstrate why reflection is as important (and as fun!) as the play experience itself.

It often works really well to allow for playful forms of expression in this part of the event, extending the play moods into the reflection session. You can do this in a variety of ways, for example, by inviting participants to reflect by building a physical manifestation of their experience using simple materials such as Play-doh, paper, cardboard or LEGO bricks.

Transforming Democracies

In this chapter, I have described my approach to designing play events that might foster playful, democratic participation. Now, the 'might' in that sentence will probably make some readers question the validity of my argument, but despite systematic effort, there is no guarantee that play will happen. The more you try to force play to happen a certain way, the more you risk that it won't happen at all.

Even *if* you manage to successfully design for a profound, memorable play experience, it remains unclear how the single event can fuel new democratic movements on a larger scale. That is one of the big, pressing questions which lies outside the scope of this chapter: what kind of connection can we identify and establish between these small, everyday acts of playful citizenship and the 'big' democracy? Is it possible to build strong bridges between the 'small' and the 'big' democracy, drawing on the spirit of play to revitalise democracy at large?

Coming back to Donatella della Porta, she demonstrates that:

'[P]articipation creates a virtuous circle' where 'opportunities to participate stimulate trust and activism, thus reproducing the stimulus to participate and improving the effects of participation itself' (della Porta 2013).

While CounterPlay may be a special place, we do not have unique skills or resources available. Hence, if we can create a space where this atmosphere thrives, then it should be possible to do the same all over society: in schools and universities, libraries, museums, urban spaces, private companies and more. With small steps, anyone can cause real change.

Quick Take-Aways

Play events can be designed to foster new forms of democratic participation.

When you design a play event, remember the three pillars: (1) Participation, (2) Embodied Deliberation and (3) Imagination. Ensure opportunities to reflect on the play experience for a bigger impact.

Consider how your play event might be a catalyst for forming a sustainable play community, and what you can do to support that.

Further Reading

Brown, S. L. (2009). *Play: How it Shapes the Brain, Opens the Imagination, and Invigorates the Soul*. Penguin.

Della Porta, D. (2013). *Can Democracy be Saved? Participation, Deliberation and Social Movements*. John Wiley & Sons.

Dunne, A. & Raby, F. (2013). *Speculative Everything: Design, Fiction, and Social Dreaming*. MIT Press.

Henricks, T. S. (2015). *Play and the Human Condition*. University of Illinois Press.

Henricks, T. (2016). Playing into the Future. *Celebrating, 40*, 169-184.

Mouffe, C. (2018). *For a left Populism*. Verso Books.

Knudsen, B. T. & Christensen, D. R. (2014). Eventful Events: Eventmaking Strategies in contemporary Culture. In *Enterprising Initiatives in the Experience Economy* (pp. 117-134). Routledge.

Poulsen, M., Langham, K., Wood, Z. & Tomlinson, D. (2017). The Power of Play – Voices from the Play Community. Retrieved at: http://counterplay.org/files/PowerOfPlay_CounterPlay.pdf

Runciman, D. (2018). *How Democracy Ends*. Profile Books.

Skovbjerg, H. M. (2016). *Perspektiver på leg*. Turbine Akademisk.

Acknowledgement

For a number of years, I have embarked on journeys that didn't have a clear destination, and I have made many silly proposals with no obvious outcome. Along the way, I have tried to focus solely on what play needs to thrive, nothing more, nothing less. I only ever found the courage to work like this because I was not alone. I am grateful and forever indebted to many people, but more than any one individual, I want to thank the play community that instill in us all the confidence that play is worth fighting and living for.

Play Design Insight 10:

Play Design Methods in Organisational Development

Sune Gudiksen

In this play design insight, we move the play scene to organisational practices and development. Play design methods are suggested as ways to move from the status quo, operational, everyday activities in organisations towards the exploration of new visionary territories. The chapter presents a model that gives the reader the understanding of which play design methods to use and for what purpose in organisational development. This is illustrated through three types of play design methods used in various organisations: (1) design thinking play, (2) innovation games, and (3) organisational dilemma games.

Introduction

In design and development processes in general, framing the 'right' problems and solution direction are often considered crucial. Acclaimed design researchers Nigel Cross and Kees Dorst (2015; 2001) have argued through empirical evidence that problem and solution follow a co-evolution throughout a development process, unlike many academic disciplines where problem questions stay the same. The ability to frame and reframe are crucial in a process where teams and/or broader circles of stakeholders are experimenting in the unknown and ultimately taking qualitative judgements based on available inputs.

In such situations, executed in a strong way, play design methods can challenge assumptions, elicit surprises, radically change perspectives and set new directions, while also creating social interactions leading to better cross-disciplinary and cross-functional relations. Such play design methods act as an activity of co-discovery of framing and reframing opportunities before entering phases with more detailed solutions.

Through carefully designed play design methods, and through the application of these in diverse organisational situations as well as studying interaction patterns, I have found over the course of ten years that this is where play and game techniques can have an influential impact on organisational development activities. Especially in those situations where the agenda is to move significantly beyond status quo operating activities and search for opportunities in unknown waters or in situations where debriefing or setting the course for new approaches are crucial.

> "The play factor can create an immersive and liberating space from everyday routines and a set of activities that allows for exploration and prioritisation of radically new opportunities."

This chapter briefly outlines how to see play design methods as an enabler of a shift in participants' orientation from status quo and ongoing operations towards an experimental space that allows for the exploration of new visionary territory.

Play Design Methods in an organisational ambidexterity Perspective

It has been thoroughly documented by global innovation thinkers that finding the balance between ongoing operations and new initiatives is key to successful operations on a leadership level (Christensen

2013; Govindarajan 2016; Govindarajan & Timble 2013; McGrath 2013). For instance, Govindarajan and colleagues describe this as an inevitable paradox that organisations cannot avoid but rather require balancing strategies. Ongoing operations are characterised by short-term thinking, repeatability, and predictability, whereas innovation is based on long-term thinking, chaos, serendipity, and unpredictability. In a nutshell, Govindarajan et al. (2016) argue that:

'Organisations are not designed for innovation. Quite the contrary, they are designed for ongoing operations'.

With temporary, rather than sustainable, advantages being the new norm, the existing value model in companies will always come under pressure, suggesting the need for reconfiguration and renewal of advantages in a more rapid pace. Here it is important to prepare new business advantages ahead of time, rather than wait till economic decline.

Ludic Spaces in Organisations

In the search for new opportunities that can lead to temporary advantages, the dilemma is that the ongoing operation constraints are difficult to work around. This chapter renounces viewing play as a romanticised phenomenon where we enter a magical world and leave everything behind. This is not what I have observed.

> "Play design methods can challenge assumptions, elicit surprises, radically change perspectives and set new directions, while also creating social interactions leading to better cross-disciplinary and cross-functional relations."

Everyday work constraints do not vanish in the air, and free play does not exist – at least not in these settings. Play in these settings also means hard work and mental fatigue because of a high degree of interaction, the use of all senses for obtaining knowledge and being immersed in exploratory activities. Two-to-three hours with play design methods results in participants having more than enough new inputs and the rest of the day can benefit from low-level energy situations. Having said this, the play factor can create an immersive and liberating space from everyday routines and a set of activities that allows for exploration and prioritisation of radically new opportunities. Ongoing operations are put on hold or somewhat suspended for a short while, but tend to pop-up occasionally in the activities. Explicitly, exploring new waters and finding unforeseen opportunities is the goal. Implicitly, social interaction and two-way communication are at the heart of the activities.

Understanding
Play Design Methods

The variety of playful methods for organisational practices are extensive but they all seem to build on five cores (see Prologue for a description of these):

(1) Metaphors/Narratives,
(2) Rules/Procedures,
(3) Materials/Technologies,
(4) Challenges/Feedback,
(5) Participation/Position.

These components govern how the play activities unfold and what players can do, all of which affect the outcomes the activities can produce. Let us take a moment to briefly investigate the relationship between structure and outcome.

There are two archetypes of play and game structures, namely a ludic-progression structure and a paidia-emergence structure. These opposites follow a long history on play research that indicates a dialectic always present in play activities (Callois 1961; Juul 2011).

The progression structure is based on sessions where the player must perform a predefined sequence of events. Often these activities are described more as games that are built around a progression structure that is usually fairly predictable because players always go through the same sequences in the same order. The progression structure yields a great deal

of control to the organisational play designer and facilitator, as he or she controls the sequences of the events. This type of game often has a strong storytelling ambition and in-depth premade content.

The emergence structure is based on a few initial structures that, when combined, generate many possible situations in the play activities. Play built around an emergence structure is usually unpredictable because patterns and possible directions combine and interact in ways no one can foresee. Where progression games can be illustrated as a straightforward staircase, emergence play and games can be viewed as a huge grid with many intersections.

It is possible to place the different type of play design methods within this spectrum. From design thinking play with few upfront rules and creative constraints to instruction games with few, if any, choices.

Now let me exemplify with three different play design methods supported by organisational case examples.

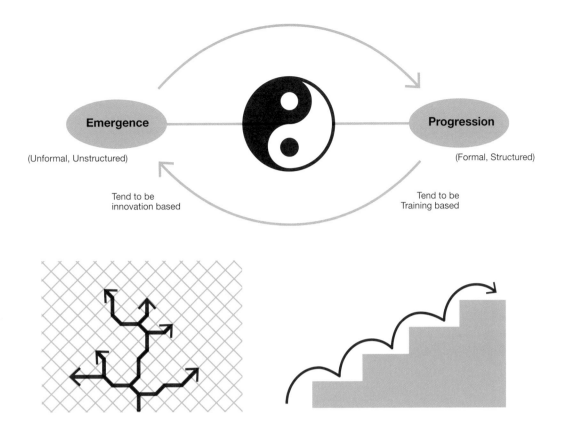

*Figure 10.1: Paidia-emergence & ludic-progression
– reworked, first appeared in Gudiksen & Inlove (2018)*

Play Method 1: Design Thinking Play

As previously mentioned, the framing and reframing in the development process are crucial. If you then add a complexity that you normally find in bigger organisations that a number of stakeholders with diverse professional backgrounds need to find common ground and work together, this task is complex and extremely difficult. In a recent article, influential design thinkers Tim Brown and Roger Martin expressed the need to initiate 'iterative interaction with the decision-makers', calling such interventions 'more critical to success than the design of the artefacts themselves' (Brown & Martin 2015). In the early stages of a development process, design thinking play and games can be used to challenge assumptions and elicit surprises that lead to re-orientation for the participants involved and, by the end of the activities, also common understanding. The balance to seek for the play designer is to create enough incentives through simple play game techniques to explore new scenarios but also to keep the activities open and follow the direction it takes. The activities usually last between 45–60 minutes and can then be put together in a three-hour workshop or similar. Here, I will give two short examples.

Stakeholder Grid Game Example

In the first case, design thinking play were used to shed light on the current understanding of the relationships among journalists, media producers, politicians and citizens (or viewers) as part of TV concept development in relation to an upcoming national parliament election. Design thinking play were also used to establish design criteria based on the interests of each stakeholder group. After these activities, the project moved to the generation of ideas about possible programme themes and angles. The participants were divided into two groups. One group focused on the media content of a channel that delivers programmes for people between 15 and 35 years old (typically programmes with concrete actions). The other group focused on the debate-related media content of a channel that delivers good debates.

We called the activity *The Stakeholder Grid Game*. The purpose was to explore, establish and prioritise design criteria, as well as to discuss the relationships among these criteria from the perspectives of the

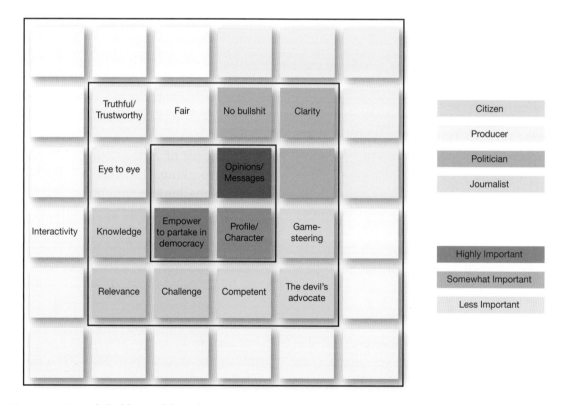

Figure 10.2: Stakeholder grid board & outcomes from DR national television case

various stakeholders. The game used a simple game board with squares, each of which represented a design criterion (Figure 10.2). By design criteria, we mean the perspectives of each stakeholder group that could lead to their participation in, contribution to and concepts of ideas that we could judge and evaluate. Writeable, transparent bricks were used so that the criteria could be easily moved around. The procedure was as follows: First, the groups were told to think only about criteria related to each of the four stakeholder categories: citizen (blue), producer (yellow),

politician (red) and journalist (green). Second, the groups discussed the criteria and positioned them according to their relative levels of importance. Hence, the game was also a prioritising activity. The inner square illustrated the most important criterion for each stakeholder to participate in a positive manner.

The two groups' chosen criteria differed in many ways. For example, for the group that focused on viewers that was interested in good discussions, the most important criterion for the citizen was to

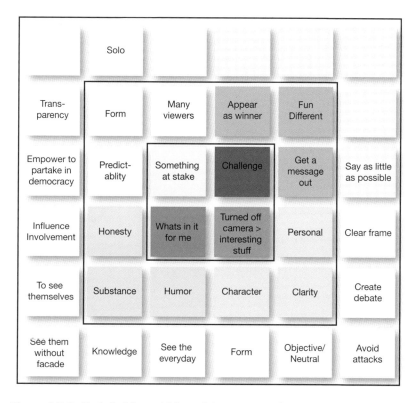

Figure 10.3: Stakeholder grid board & outcomes from DR national television case

'empower to partake in democracy' (see Figure 10.2, blue corner); however, this criterion was seriously challenged by the other group, which saw 'what's in it for me' as the most important criterion for the citizen. Both groups began to question their own criteria.

From activities early on focusing on establishing design criteria, the participants can then move on to generate ideas and scenarios. In such a design stage, iterations on various scenarios, and consider pros and cons helps to evaluate these up against each other. For this purpose, I have used two different design thinking plays – Pinball customer flow and Domino value chain – that allow for a high degree of open-ended scenario-making but also triggers new scenarios to appear outside of the radar of the participants, in order to propel them out of habitual thinking and status quo understanding of the world, and into imaginative modes where participants search for new scenarios and new meaning.

Pinball Customer Flow Example

Figure 10.4 depict how participants from a large Amusement park were discussing and building up in the pinball game scenarios down the ramp related to introducing a new digital bracelet as access point for visitors to know for instance cue time, best places to go in the park and similar wayfinding challenges. In around 45 min they developed 3-4 different scenarios they can

Figure 10.4: Pinball customer flow example – amusement park

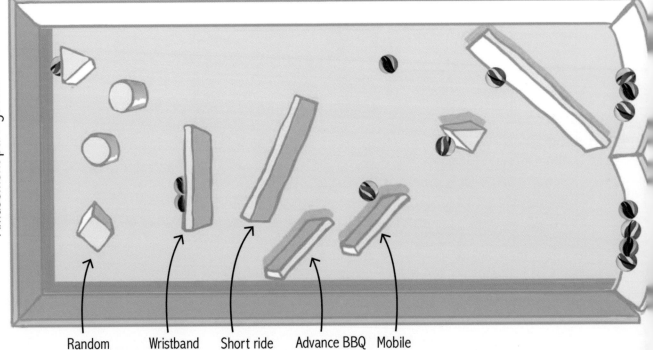

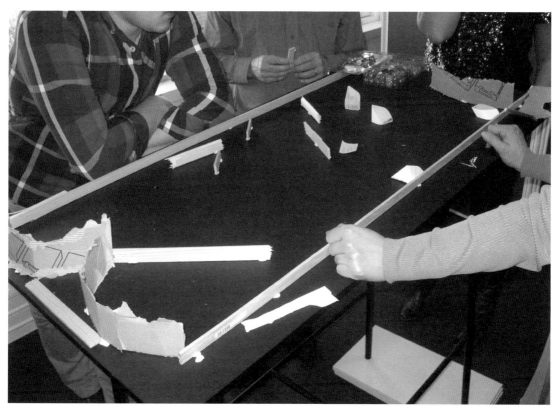

Figure 10.5: Pinball customer flow game – touchpoints and barriers being placed

then evaluate up against each other and decide on best part to work further with. The pinball game works both as a shared communication early prototype and a way to work through a specific concept with various scenarios in play. Often prototypes in design challenge assumptions by the very making of it, but in this case it is both the making part and the try-out of the balls – a double action, first you need to reach common understanding and then you have to act upon a randomizer incident.

Domino Value Chain Structuring

Another example is an activity we call Domino value chain, which has been ap-

plied in several situations with SME companies looking for new ways to structure their value chain and in a participatory setting challenge current structures and ideate on new ones. Like in the Pinball game participants create the domino content and place each value chain part as they understand the status quo. A dice roll challenges participants to take certain actions like switching around two random dominoes; removing a domino or adding in-between dominoes activating participants to think in new, potentially better structures.

The Pinball and Domino activities are simple but can have a surprisingly striking

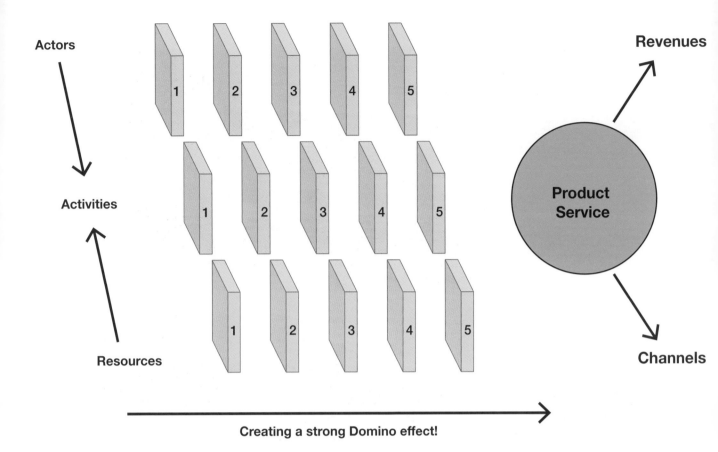

Creating a strong Domino effect!

Figure 10.6: Pictures 1-2: Domino value chain game

effect on the participants framing of a specific scenario. Most of the content is created on the day through ideation before the pinball and domino activities, and then scenarios are created and tested in these activities. Some boundaries are created on beforehand like for instance in the Pinball game what are ending points for customers or in the Domino game what the overall elements could be for instance actors, activities and resources. As facilitator one needs to encourage participants to build and test in iterations in order to make the thinking concrete.

Play Design Method 2: Innovation Games

With innovation games, we move towards a method which has more structure, predefined tasks and theory incorporated into the core of the game activities. The innovation game *Business model branching* deals with the difficult and complex challenge of balancing ongoing operations and new innovation-oriented activities, a.k.a. organisational ambidexterity, as described in the beginning.

It is of vital importance for all companies to constantly work on finding this balance through resource allocation, competence development, and generally understanding the need for both parts of the dilemma to be present in everyday business situations.

Therefore, it is crucial for companies to build up a portfolio of new visionary business opportunities, so they can avoid significant declines in profit when specific markets are disrupted – or maybe even profit from seeking business opportunities progressively. Consequently, leaders, managers, developers and designers need to learn how to balance the resource allocation between ongoing operations and innovation. The purpose of this game is to exercise the ability to allocate resources to *launch* and *ramp up* concrete new business branches, while also exploiting, reconfiguring, and disengaging the old business branches.

Gameplay: Moving Upward and Sideways

The game consists of a centre board and up to eight possible branches. The centre board includes the 'Why' with a reference to Simon Sinek's (2011) golden circle. Variations can be written into this 'why' based on how new branches provoke new aspects of the 'why'. The 'why' and vision of a company is always emerging when it comes to specific interpretations, either dealt with explicitly or as a movement forced by market changes. The branches illustrate value proposition cycles on a scale: (1) Launch, (2) Ramp up, (3) Exploit, (4) Reconfigure, and (5) Disengage. Participants are challenged both to move upstream and sideways. Challenges related to upstream movement relate to each stage in the value cycle. A variety of

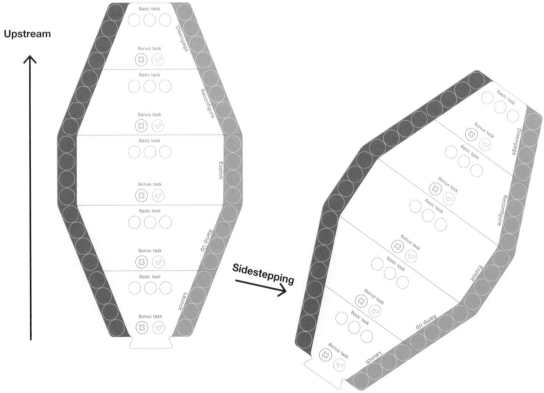

Figure 10.7: Pictures 1-2: Business model branching board & upstream/side-stepping principles

competencies, instantiations, and strategies are needed for each stage. Participants have basic tasks to fulfil and bonus tasks that provide extra resources and movements in subsequent rounds.

Sideways movement marks a transition from one branch to another. Here, the participants have to devise resources and also place people either in the red zone (in need of competence development) or in the green zone (ready to fulfil tasks). As McGrath (2013) mentions, 'another factor in play in companies that can move from one set of advantages to another is that they consciously set out to educate and up-skill their people'.

The game lets groups of participants work with the basic tasks for minutes to hours based on the time available and then return to the board to discuss changes related to both the 'why' of the company as well as the specific balance between ongoing operations and innovation. Based on McGrath's theory, Business model branching has a scoring algorithm that pressures participants to launch new branches before old branches die out or else they face the same destiny as companies in the real market – going bankrupt. This helps participants look further into their future than their current business branches, while also letting them see that they shouldn't launch new initiatives all the time. It strikes the balance between being overly enamoured with existing value proposi-

tions to launch something new launching too many new value propositions without having the necessary resources and the right competencies in place.

Marketing and Promotion Company Case

In a case clearly illustrating the paradox between ongoing operations and innovation, we worked with a company that had years of success on their existing value proposition based on promotion and marketing. Now, they experienced the first declines and signs that reconfiguration and disengagement were not that far away, but they also found that maybe a scaling up on an existing business branch might lead to better times.

Based on this initial mapping of Business Branching, the team had identified existing value propositions and new potential business branches. Subsequently, the team was divided into two groups. One group focused on an existing business branch and how to scale this in fierce competition (upstream movement on the existing branch). The other group focused on a new value proposition of 'outdoor promotion events' (sidestep movement to a new branch). The groups went through a series of idea generation activities to further unfold the potential of each branch and then returned to discuss what these potential moves would mean for status quo practices in the company.

Based on the game, the team concluded that they currently used all their energy on a declining business branch without advancing on new business branches. Resources were needed to experiment and test new business branches – and quickly, since they were currently falling behind competitors in, for instance, digital solution promotions. Also, employees had to quickly gain new competencies related to the new business branches, while there were still resources available and time to gain them.

In many ways, this case illustrates the paradox between ongoing operations (existing value propositions and practices) and innovation (identifying and launching new value propositions). It is not an either/or approach but rather a balancing activity for leaders and employees. For this reason, it is also of vital importance that this perspective is not geared only toward leaders but also developers, designers and marketers so that everyone understands that moving from one competitive advantage to another is happening at a rapid pace.

The value of the game lies in the concrete action in upstream flows and side-stepping moves, as well as in learning about how to master this balance. The timing in the movement of resources and competence development is the key in the game and in developing temporary competitive advantages on a regular basis. Participants accelerate new insights on how to take action moves right after completing the activity based on the concrete situation they are in; thus, they learn how to manage the crucial balance.

Play Design Method 3: Dilemma Game

Dilemma games have a strong impact in situations where loosely defined, abstract business concepts and a number of cross-functional stakeholders are gathered. The purpose is to create two-way communication on horizontal and vertical levels in organisations. For instance, organisational culture, organisational values, or any other broader strategic agenda in a larger organisation can be better tackled in hands-on dilemma games rather than through one-way management presentations. Often initiated by top management in an organisation, such agendas have a hard time coming alive with management at a distance.

Case example: Rekindling Organisational Values in a Large Corporate Company

The organisational value communication challenge was the starting point in a case with a large Nordic company who offers value propositions mainly related to payment solutions of various kinds.

Why the Game Creation was Initiated

As part of a larger strategy rollout, the top management was eager to rekindle their organisational values – this time with a greater impact. The value-set outlined by the management was based on a set of 'positive' approaches to the values, that is, values that the company would like to be known for, and also a set of 'negative' approaches to the values to be avoided as much as possible.

In this case, the game was first used in a meeting with the top management and team leaders just before events related to the rekindling of the values took place. This was followed by the teams playing the game at a time of their own choosing and at special cross-division events through conference calls.

Play Design Considerations

As play designers, we were given a set of design criteria that we had to work with. The activity should be simple and easy to learn. The game should be easy to distribute and preferably printable for each team leader. As well, the game had to somehow be playable across departments and units in various countries, that is, at a distance, which meant that we needed to work with a blended version including both physical and digital elements.

We created a game board with hexagonal markers. Each of these contained a specific

Redefining ACT to support cultural change ...

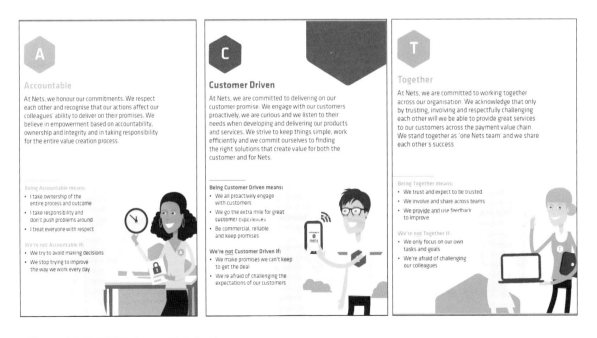

Figure 10.8: NETS three official values

dilemma. In this game, the participants all played together and competed against the board. This created collaboration between participants and led to a shared enemy. When dealing with the dilemmas, the participants had to follow three simple steps:

(1) Analysing the dilemma based on factors that could turn values into a negative source. They gave scores from 0 to 3.
(2) Generate one or two approaches.
(3) Evaluate the approach against positive values. They gave scores from 0 to 1.

In this way, the participants earned points through working with the dilemmas. From the outer A series, the participants could then move into the next series and ultimately reach the 'grand dilemmas' by the end. The complexity and the difficulty rose when they moved to the next series. In sixty minutes, the participants played through eight to nine dilemmas, and each time they needed to address the values.

To enable a play possibility across borders and from a distance, an interactive slide-show was created with all the dilemma descriptions and the dice. Therefore, the only two things to print were the board and a single game brick.

The game ends when the participants have been through eight or nine dilemmas or beaten the board score (see Figure 10.10). After this, the groups could compare approaches and discuss how they experienced the dialogue around the dilemmas and the chosen approaches.

Applied Game Dialogue Examples
While playing the game, participants would have to go through a dialogue process containing the aforementioned three steps in a chronological way following the game structure.

This dialogue created a solution customised to fit the participants' own understanding and working experience. At the same time, the dialogue created shared communica-

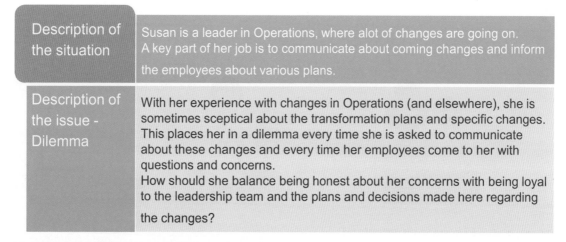

Description of the situation	Susan is a leader in Operations, where alot of changes are going on. A key part of her job is to communicate about coming changes and inform the employees about various plans.
Description of the issue - Dilemma	With her experience with changes in Operations (and elsewhere), she is sometimes sceptical about the transformation plans and specific changes. This places her in a dilemma every time she is asked to communicate about these changes and every time her employees come to her with questions and concerns. How should she balance being honest about her concerns with being loyal to the leadership team and the plans and decisions made here regarding the changes?

Figure 10.9: A dilemma example & scoring system

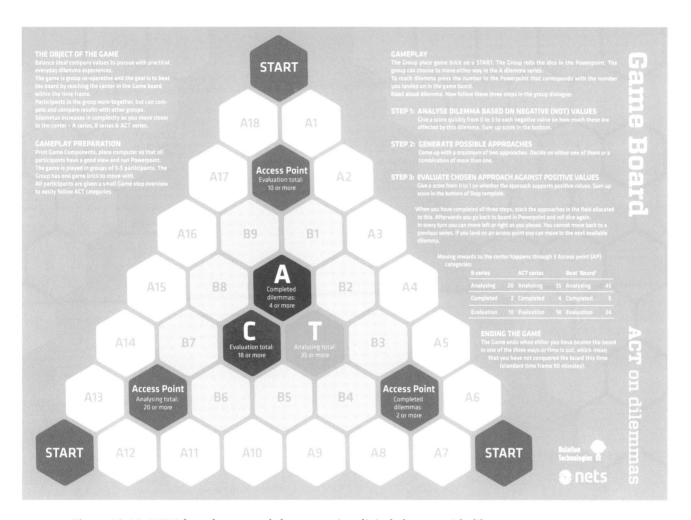

Figure 10.10: NETS board game and the supporting digital element with dilemmas

tion about different work experiences and forced compromises fitted to various dilemma context since participants are sharing specifics from their own everyday working situations. If the dilemma does not represent participants' working context, we observed that they instead practised and exchanged ideas about the specifics around the context of the dilemma.

In the evaluation part of the game, participants were reinforcing the elements of the company values. In this phase of the game,

we saw that the perceptions of behaviour came into play. Participants tested their perception of a specific behaviour embraced in the company values in a shared narrative of the context of the dilemma. This process and dialogue created a wider understanding of the context of the dilemma and behaviour behind a value.

The Head of HR development at NETS afterwards expressed the outcome in this way:

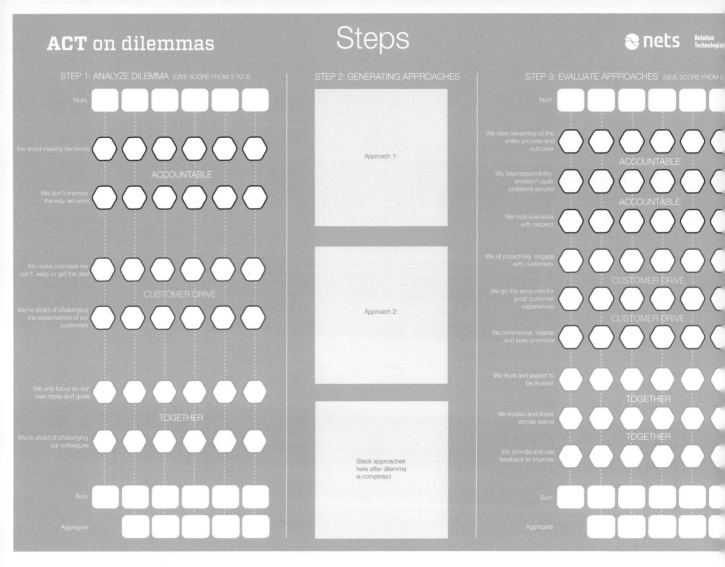

Figur 10.11: Steps and scoring mechanism in dilemma game

'The game has given us three things: A new and different way to work with values that engage people. The participants are walked through the values and their meaning again, and again, and after only one hour they remembered the essence of the values. Finally, the game contributes to both unlearning and acquiring of the behaviour we wish to cultivate in NETS in order to strengthen our company culture'.

Overall, the process secured and created a structured dialogue with a clear focus on the company set of values in relation to specific everyday dilemma situations.

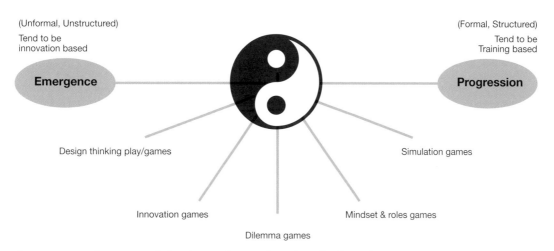

Figure 10.12: Placement of the glay and game-based methods in the emergence-progression spectrum

Quick Take-Aways

In all the play design methods described, the play flow advances in steps; however, there is a variation in how fixed these are and, in the way, a particular paidia-ludic space is constrained (toward progression) or deconstrained (toward emergence) from the start and along the way. The two game structures presented earlier (see Figure 2) are extremes. Many play and game activities have elements of both progression and emergence, where sequences of events are predetermined while there is simultaneously room in each step to enable multiple scenarios. What is interesting about how these structures relate to these activities is that the choice of play structure has a close connection to the outcomes each activity seeks to produce. If the purpose is competence development, the play or game structure usually leans toward progression structures. These games are also based on premade content based on theory or observations experienced over time. If the purpose is primarily organisational development, the game structure usually leans toward emergence structures, wherein some content is created beforehand, but most of it is created through gameplay like in the design thinking play examples. Some of the play activities can be used for both competence development and organisational development, but even in this case, one purpose is still prioritised higher than the other.

Further Reading

Brandt, E. (2006). Designing exploratory Design Games: a Framework for Participation in Participatory Design? *Proceedings from Proceedings of the Ninth Conference on Participatory Design: Expanding Boundaries in Design – Volume 1.*

Brown, T., & Martin, R. (2015). Design for Action. *Harvard business review Sep2015*, 93(9), 56-64.

Caillois, R. (1961). *Man, Play, and Games.* University of Illinois Press.

Dorst, K., & Cross, N. (2001). Creativity in the Design Process: Co-evolution of Problem–solution. Design Studies, 22(5), 425-437.

Dorst, K. (2015). *Frame Innovation: Create New Thinking by Design.* MIT Press.

Christensen, C. M. (2013). *The Innovator's Dilemma: when New Technologies cause great Firms to Fail.* Harvard Business Review Press.

Govindarajan, V., & Trimble, C. (2010). *The other Side of Innovation: Solving the Execution Challenge.* Harvard Business Press.

Govindarajan, V. (2016). *The Three-Box Solution: A Strategy for Leading Innovation.* Harvard Business Review Press.

Gudiksen, S. (2015). Business Model Design Games: Rules and Procedures to challenge Assumptions and Elicit Surprises. *Creativity and Innovation Management*, 24(2), 307-322.

Gudiksen, S. & Inlove, J. (2018). *Gamification for Business – Why Innovators and Changemakers use Games to Break down Silos, Drive Engagement and Build Trust.* Kogan Page. London.

Juul, J. (2011). *Half-real: Video Games between Real Rules and Fictional Worlds.* MIT press.

McGrath, R. G. (2013). *The End of competitive Advantage: How to Keep your Strategy Moving as Fast as your Business.* Harvard Business Review Press.

Sinek, S. (2009). *Start with why: How Great Leaders Inspire Everyone to Take Action.* Penguin.

Acknowledgement

I would like to thank the students involved in the projects and company Actee especially Leif Sørensen for the co-development of the NETS game.

Epilogue

The Future of Play Design

Sune Gudiksen & Helle Marie Skovbjerg

Congratulations, you reached the epilogue! – whether through skimming, reading it all or jumping directly to the end. We hope the chapters gave you ideas and principles to inspire or encourage play activities in your world. In this epilogue, we highlight what we believe to be some future directions in the field of play design.

Such future orientations also derive from our engagement and dialogue with students in our Master's programme in play design and the network of practitioner and researcher peers that is quickly developing. The students will play a key role in further expanding and broadening play design in society at large. Descriptions of future directions are therefore best illustrated by short examples of some of the first projects by Master's students.

This epilogue should not be regarded as the conclusion of a systematic study documented in detail, but rather as a conversation starter or a kind of blueprint for the future. While the boiling pot metaphor in the Prologue works as a first recipe for play design, this chapter may serve to stimulate imaginative cooks (that means you) to create new and exciting dishes.

Naturally, therefore, the ideas and recommendations here are subject to further development through play activities experienced and observed, as well as through conversations with communities of practitioners and researchers.

Master Programme Design-for-Play

The Master's Design-for-play programme relies on a play design pedagogy incorporating a high degree of student-centred learning and a focus on concrete design proposals, as well as design anthropology and participatory design approaches throughout. In general, education is shifting from the traditional one-way communication within a classroom (mostly consisting of presentations by a teacher) to two-way communication, where the learning happens in the continuous development of a concrete play design and in dialogue with a variety of experienced supervisors, skilled lab workshop managers and specific stakeholders, all often taking place outside of the classroom. By this means, the Master's course develops graduates who are capable of both participating in cross-disciplinary teams that develop design solutions on a practical level and at the same time challenging organisational and societal practices and inspiring future directions through new play design concepts and processes.

Play is for All, not only the Few

The Design-for-play group does not treat play as a phenomenon that belongs to or occurs only in a certain age, at a specific time in our life or in a few specific contexts. It has consistently been documented that being exposed to and allowed to play results in better coping mechanisms and a more balanced mindset and attitude throughout life. Thus, play must not be confined to a time or place but rather opened up for all, and in every possible context.

Our collaboration partner, the LEGO Foundation, aims to support developing countries with funding or systems for introducing or encouraging play. Even in – or especially in – countries where life is hard, play can be the one single factor that gives people a reason to carry on. We have had students in collaboration with the LEGO Foundation creating play designs that take their point of departure in local cultures and materials. These designs are re-playable in two ways: (1) the same players may build more and more activities into the play experience, and (2) the play design and the materials may be re-used many times by other players.

Former students Cinzia Damonte and Beate Neimane were collaborating with local partners in South Africa and the LEGO Foundation in low-income and semi-rural areas. They developed a simple but highly relevant and easy usable play design for educational use, consisting of a container, 10 bottle 'counters' (bottle caps) and a play activity book describing 80 suggested activities, put into categories and with guidelines. The bottle caps are some of the most commonly used everyday items in low-income schools and semi-rural areas, and they are (re)used for multiple purposes. Former students Laura Ospina and Signe Neustrup likewise worked with the LEGO Foundation and with local partners in Colombia to encourage playful learning and, in cooperation with teachers, to get the most out of the local materials and the classroom spaces.

Investigations of the use of various materials has for long been a part of design development. As many of the chapters in this book indicate, a deep understanding of materials' capability and affordances is important. Depending on disciplines and contexts, objects, items and the spatial environment will differ. However, the 'finish' of specific designs often varies considerably: it might not always be stylish or aesthetically pleasing and wrapped in a beautiful package. This is an attractive aspect for some participants, but others may be reluctant to turn a design into their own and change it as they like. Therefore, play design to a high degree combines object-based design (industrial, textile, wearable) and interactive design (interaction between human and object or between human and human and the object). In future, design must consider interaction and participant-led play, including re-playability and the re-use of materials, objects and spaces. We argue that social and sustainability agendas can be further initiated and fostered within such considerations.

This means that play design and play design research cannot be confined within specific boundaries or that play design outcomes have a specific generic form – which could undeniably be easier to handle. Hence, we aim to insert play design into all sorts of applied contexts and life situations where play has the potential to do good for people. We invite you to take part in this movement.

Curious and Imaginative Human Beings

Play has a clear connection to exploration, which inevitably overlaps with creativity. Play in general usually means chaotic and messy activities, whether involving one or a few players or in bigger community settings. Vice versa play might not be a strong activity when daily operations and chores kick-in, unless one wants to disrupt and challenge these. We hope that participants in play will wish to keep on asking and posing questions, rather than seeking specific answers in advance.

If there are any learning goals to pursue in play design, they should be related to the ability to be curious on our learning journey through life and to give rein to our imagination. Play can serve as an important impetus to challenge our worldview or that of others, gradually and sometimes radically. Being exposed to surprises through triggers and prompts leads to a curious mindset. A number of students in the Master's programme and researchers in the Design-for-play group have explored various ways to create alternative scenarios of play, by combining and arranging spatial conditions or through the metaphorical staging of play; sometimes these scenarios are speculative–investigative, sometimes critical and sometimes directly and immediately applicable in large community settings. Former students Rebecca Houmøller and Neza Landeker developed playful ways to engage participants in workshops, using all sorts of materials, sounds, video and staging techniques to stimulate future scenarios. Former students Keila Quinones and Maria Vitaller del Olmo used so-called play probes that intervened in ordinary practices of eating and drinking, participants are given an excuse or a motivation to bring sensitive topics like immigration, feminism, education and climate change among other public policy topics to the table. In this they argue that play has an important role as it alleviates much of the pressure these topics may bring with them, encouraging opinion-building and equal participation.

Design-for-play group members Pia Schytz and Sune Gudiksen have experimented with objects and metaphorical play staging in workshops, with a view to rejecting status quo operations and moving towards the creation of new meaning. These approaches are gaining momentum. While politicians use metaphors to frame messages to the public, play designers can use them as a means of staging a different reality, allowing the participants to suspend situational and institutional constraints for a while.

Such play design can assist in developing people to continuously challenge assumptions and see problems and issues from various angles, including the angle of the person sitting opposite. We could call this play design thinking – promoting people's curiosity and imagination and their ability to reframe societal and life challenges at a more rapid pace.

While this can be a 'daring' way of living, participants cannot go beyond their limits in terms of preferences and skills if they are not ready to do so. Perhaps the finest role of the play design facilitator or play experience facilitator in any situation is to understand each player and the extent to which he or she can and wants to be involved. Small steps seen from the outside may be bigger steps for someone on the 'inside'. Although deploying such sensitivity to the needs and wishes of all in complex play activities with a high number of players is extremely difficult, this is still the aim.

The future of play design must not seek to formalise play in the interest of pre-defined learning outcomes. Play is not only about the players but also seeks to advance their thinking, providing inspirational triggers and prompts that will lead to new circles of imagination. The characteristics and wonders of unknown outcomes will be lost if the rules are strict and cannot be changed, adapted or adjusted. We suggest that play designers strive to find a good balance between progression and emergent patterns, between the orderly and the unruly and between rules and spontaneity in practical play design. If play designers and researchers carefully observe interactions from more open-ended play we are sure a conglomerate of various plays can be found and be further explored, categorized and used for inspiration to new play designs.

Agency and Activism
Play design in future will necessarily entail the empowerment and agency of the players, letting them influence why and how they play. As a designer, one cannot only be content with the systems that one inherits – being a change agent is part of the DNA. For the play designer, social interactions are central. Both in design and in research, play designers should dare to be activists, creating interventions, observing interactions and keeping detailed

records in order to explore alternative futures and comparing these with present day practices.

This might also mean a re-orientation in the play products industry towards more open-ended and re-usable play that offers participants a greater degree of imaginative possibilities and agency in terms of acting independently and making choices of their own. Thus, we encourage more players to become play-makers, not only in any specific play activity but by developing inquisitiveness, creativity and boldness that spill over into all aspects of life.

Let us continue the play design conversation!

Feel free to contact Design-for-play Group:

skg@dskd.dk

hms@dskd.dk

List of Figures